XDA Developers' Android™ Hacker's Toolkit

XDA Developers' Android™ Hacker's Toolkit

THE COMPLETE GUIDE TO ROOTING, ROMS AND THEMING

Jason Tyler with Will Verduzco

This work is a co-publication between XDA Developers and John Wiley & Sons, Ltd.

A John Wiley and Sons, Ltd, Publication

This edition first published 2012
© 2012 John Wiley and Sons, Ltd.

Registered office
John Wiley & Sons Ltd, The Atrium, Southern Gate, Chichester, West Sussex,
PO19 8SQ, United Kingdom

For details of our global editorial offices, for customer services and for
information about how to apply for permission to reuse the copyright material
in this book please see our website at www.wiley.com.

The right of the author to be identified as the author of this work has been
asserted in accordance with the Copyright, Designs and Patents Act 1988.

All rights reserved. No part of this publication may be reproduced, stored in a
retrieval system, or transmitted, in any form or by any means, electronic,
mechanical, photocopying, recording or otherwise, except as permitted by the
UK Copyright, Designs and Patents Act 1988, without the prior permission of
the publisher.

Wiley also publishes its books in a variety of electronic formats. Some content
that appears in print may not be available in electronic books.

Designations used by companies to distinguish their products are often claimed
as trademarks. All brand names and product names used in this book are trade
names, service marks, trademarks or registered trademarks of their respective
owners. The publisher is not associated with any product or vendor mentioned
in this book. This publication is designed to provide accurate and authoritative
information in regard to the subject matter covered. It is sold on the understanding that the publisher is not engaged in rendering professional services. If
professional advice or other expert assistance is required, the services of a
competent professional should be sought.

Trademarks: Wiley and the Wiley logo are trademarks or registered trademarks of John Wiley and Sons, Inc. and/ or its affiliates in the United States
and/or other countries, and may not be used without written permission.
Android is a trademark of Google, Inc. All other trademarks are the property
of their respective owners. John Wiley & Sons, Ltd. is not associated with any
product or vendor mentioned in the book.

XDA, XDA Developers is a trademark of JB Online Media, LLC
A catalogue record for this book is available from the British Library.

ISBN 978-1-119-95138-4 (paperback); ISBN 978-1-119-96154-3 (ebook);
978-1-119-96155-0 (ebook); 978-1-119-96156-7 (ebook)

Set in 9.5/11.5 Minion Pro Regular by Indianapolis Composition Services

Printed in the United States by Courier Westford

R0440165137

PUBLISHER'S ACKNOWLEDGEMENTS

Some of the people who helped bring this book to market include the following:

Editorial and Production
VP Consumer and Technology Publishing Director: Michelle Leete
Associate Director–Book Content Management: Martin Tribe
Associate Publisher: Chris Webb
Assistant Editor: Ellie Scott
Development Editor: Shena Deuchars
Copy Editor: Shena Deuchars
Technical Editor: Akshay Dashrath
Editorial Manager: Jodi Jensen
Senior Project Editor: Sara Shlaer
Editorial Assistant: Leslie Saxman

Marketing
Associate Marketing Director: Louise Breinholt
Senior Marketing Executive: Kate Parrett

Composition Services
Compositor: Indianapolis Composition Services
Proofreader: Linda Seifert
Indexer: Estalita Slivoskey

About the Authors

Jason Tyler has been an IT instructor and is currently Director of Technology for Typefrag.com. An avid Android hacker, Jason has been rooting and ROMing every Android phone he can get his hands on since the OG Droid.

Will Verduzco is a Johns Hopkins University graduate in neuroscience and is now currently studying to become a physician. He is also Portal Administrator for XDA-Developers, and has been addicted to mobile technology since the HTC Wizard. Starting with the Nexus One, however, his gadget love affair has shifted to Google's little green robot.

Contents

Foreword

The XDA Developers (XDA) website was opened in 2003. Nine years may not seem like that long ago, but Facebook wasn't even a thing then. The iPhone and the first Android handset weren't released until 2007. So, in Internet time, XDA is old. In smartphone time, we're ancient.

`xda-developers.com` is a strange URL—not as imaginative, short or catchy as most high-traffic sites. There's a simple reason for this: the site wasn't created for you. We never envisioned a smartphone revolution—or if we did, we never envisioned that millions would care so much about what was happening on our little developer-focused forum.

XDA was created for developers and it is still a site for developers. They are incredibly smart, generally selfless, and hard-working individuals who share their creations (for free) with the world. When they see a book like this, they get concerned that their site will be overrun (more than it already is) by "newbs" with annoying questions and demands. They see the title of this book—with that overused "H"-word—and roll their eyes.

So, why did XDA lend its name to this guide? Honestly? It's because we can't stop you all from coming and we'd rather you be a bit better educated when you arrive. People spend more time touching their phones than their spouses and many of those people want their phones to be completely customizable (even as their spouses are generally not). They want to remove restrictions placed on the devices by carriers and OEMs and make the phone *theirs*.

This book was written by a member of XDA. His goal was to share his enthusiasm about what he found on the site and across the Internet about the customizability of the Android operating system, to get you just as excited, and to show you the tools you need to put that excitement into action. As with most tech-related books, much of the text herein is outdated by the time it hits the shelves. But that's OK. Even if the content is slightly stale, even if you don't have any of the devices listed in the tutorial chapters, we still urge you to read it carefully so that you are better prepared to understand as you explore XDA for your device.

As a site for developers, XDA's goal is to make sure you have you respect for all those who have blazed the trail to make all this good stuff possible. We want you to use XDA responsibly—read everything before posting, understand the risks of rooting and customizing your device, and, as you learn, become a helpful, contributing member of the community.

The XDA Admin Team

Introduction

There's a reason most Android geeks have such disdain for the other major smartphone operating system. The iPhone shackles the user, with its closed source code and ecosystem ruled with an iron fist. Android, on the other hand, frees developers to tear apart and rebuild nearly every aspect of the user's experience with the operating system. Beyond the world of developer-created applications (apps), there is a vast universe of deeper customizations—custom kernels and ROMs, themes, CPU overclocks, and more.

In most cases, these tasks begin with gaining "root" access to your device. The goal of this book is to get you comfortable with the tools and vocabulary of Android hacking, to get you in the "root" mindset, and to point you towards the best online resources for expanding your knowledge even further.

FIRST THINGS FIRST: WHAT IS XDA?

The XDA Developers (XDA) website, at `http://www.xda-developers.com`, is the largest smartphone community on the Internet. As the name implies, the site—launched in 2003—is a destination for developers. "XDA" was a line of phones based on Windows Mobile that were branded by O2 and developed by a small (at the time) Taiwanese manufacturer called High Tech Computer Corporation (HTC). According to XDA history:

> It was these early O2 XDA devices that the founders of our site thought had much more potential than the sellers O2 and HTC were giving them credit for. With their geeky hats on they cracked them open and began to develop them beyond the standard fairly boring branded versions. To spread the word, they set up a small website and naturally called it xda-developers. In the early days they had less than a dozen members (2003).

As more and more phones were released, the XDA administrators launched a new forum for each one. The site was built around the spirit of community and cooperation. XDA itself is not an organization of developers. The site is merely a sandbox where developers congregate.

From those early few members, XDA became known as the go-to source for information on how to make phones do more great stuff and how to fix a phone that was otherwise broken. As more people were attracted to the site, enthusiasts were given a home to share the awesomeness of mobile device development. From that early core of a few dozen enthusiasts, geeks and developers, the XDA website now receives more than ten million visitors per month and thousands of informative posts every day.

The material in this book draws heavily on the work done by the fantastic community at XDA. The book combines the work of the XDA community, my technical teaching experience, and my work as an Android developer to provide a launching point for the budding Android hacker.

The XDA forums have become the foremost Internet destination for information about mobile devices: how to fix them, how to hack them and, generally, how to make them better than the manufacturers make them. http://forum.xda-developers.com is laid out in forums dedicated to individual devices. Each forum contains a core group of people who work with and love the device, as well as thousands of helpful individuals on the same journey as you. When you visit XDA, you can use the "Forums" link and navigate through the forums to find your specific device (see Figure 1).

Figure 1: The device-specific forums at http://forum.xda-developers.com

THE DRAGONS THAT LIE AHEAD

The freedom offered to you when your device is rooted is liberating. It affords you such wonders as:

- complete backup of all applications and their data
- Google Apps, if they were not included with your device
- overclocking your device (speeding it up to run faster and better)
- fixing manufacturer issues, such as GPS errors or call dropping
- wireless tethering to create a quickie "hotspot"
- completely changing and customizing the device interface.

All of this and more is available to those who step out on a limb and root their Android device. However, there are two caveats to keep in mind before you get started.

You should know before you read any further that by even thinking about rooting your device you may have voided your warranty.

Not really, of course, but attempting any of the customizations that you read about in this book will void your manufacturer's warranty and any insurance warranty you may have purchased. Manufacturers and mobile service carriers sell millions of devices every week. For every device they sell, they have to support a certain percentage of those devices that are defective. As far as your carrier and OEM are concerned, when you mess with the stuff they have spent millions on making, their responsibility to support you ends.

There are no exceptions to this rule. Most OEMs, carriers and support companies will instantly reject any sort of support or replacement request when they find the device has had its software, firmware or hardware altered outside normal parameters. Even so-called "developer" devices, such as the Nexus range, cease to be supported when you start developing on them.

The second big catch is that you can do permanent irreversible damage to your device. In the parlance of the mobile device hacker, this is known as "bricking" because it turns your $400 smartphone into something as useful as a brick. Some of the exploits that are used to gain "root" access are edge-of-the-knife procedures that can completely ruin a device if the tiniest mistake is made.

Some devices are more robust than others and are less likely to be bricked. The original Motorola Droid from Verizon, for instance, was known for being almost impossible to permanently brick. But even the venerable Droid has been bricked by hasty or extremely adventurous hackers.

Many of this book's tutorials, whether to achieve root or other customizations, require you to be familiar with a command prompt window, such as the one shown in Figure 2. If you are a typical Windows user, you probably do not have much experience with the command line. Although you can find shortcuts, scripts, and workarounds, I still recommend you get comfortable with the command line. By the time you make it through Chapter 4, you'll be a command prompt pro.

Figure 2: The command prompt window

Most of the steps in this book assume that you have the ability to connect your device to your computer and that your computer has all the drivers it needs to communicate with your device. If you are unsure of this, you may need to read through Appendix A to get your phone connected to your computer. Your best shot at getting your particular device connected to your computer is to do a quick search of the XDA forums to locate the drivers. Don't do all the hard work of locating the right drivers if one of the wonderful people at XDA has already located them.

The other dragon that can gobble up the new hacker is that most Android device hacking requires the Software Development Kit (SDK) to be installed on your computer. In Appendix A, I walk you through setting up the Android SDK and point out the few pieces that you actually need for hacking your Android device.

For many devices, much of the risk has been removed by developers and hackers who have created scripts, one-click methods, and helper tools to root and customize your device. The XDA forums are an awesome community of curious and extremely intelligent people that can get you out of most dead ends when hacking your phone.

In order to access the wealth of information undoubtedly available for your device, you must first navigate to your device-specific forum. Finding the dedicated forum for your device is a simple task that can be accomplished several ways. While you could comb through the forum index and find your device manually, this can become quite frustrating given the extremely large number of device forums.

An easier method to find your device-specific forum is to use the "Find Your Device" box in the upper-right hand corner of the screen, see Figure 3 (top). Simply type the name of your device, or even a few letters, and you will be presented with a list of all matching device forums. Alternatively, you can jump to devices from a particular manufacturer by using the "Devices by OS or Manufacturer" drop-down menu at the top center of the page, see Figure 3 (bottom).

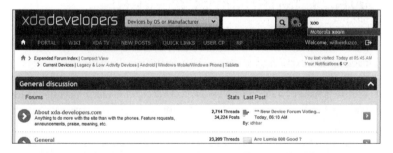

Figure 3: Searching for your device by name (top) or by manufacturer (bottom)

If you decide to continue to root your device, customize it and slip the surly bonds of OEM tyranny, you must proceed at your own risk. You have to accept the very real possibility that you could do your device permanent harm or even brick it. John Wiley & Sons, XDA Developers and I are not responsible if you turn a beautiful shiny Android device into the most expensive paperweight ever.

You have been warned.

WHO THIS BOOK IS FOR

This book is for the Android user who wants to get started with hacking Android devices. If you have heard of "rooting" an Android device and wonder what it means and how it is done, then this book is for you. This book is also for the user who wants to get more out of their Android device and increase its life and functionality.

WHAT THIS BOOK COVERS

This book covers general Android knowledge and mobile device concepts. It also includes chapters that give the reader the skills necessary to begin hacking and exploring on their own. It covers installing the tools needed, such as the Android SDK. Later chapters cover the rooting procedures for specific devices. Although devices, and Android itself, change very quickly, reading a walkthrough can prepare you for what you can expect in rooting your device.

HOW THIS BOOK IS STRUCTURED

This book is divided into two parts. The first part gives a basic overview of Android and the shell. Shell command skills will be the core of your Android-hacking career. The second part gives example walkthroughs on representative devices, from the very tightly locked to the wide open. Some devices from major manufacturers are given a detailed walkthrough to demonstrate how the skills learned earlier can be applied. The appendix walks you through getting your computing environment set up to hack Android.

WHAT YOU NEED TO USE THIS BOOK

You need a PC with Windows (XP or later), a free USB port (USB hubs are not generally recommended), and an Internet connection. You need to be familiar with navigating the XDA forums in order to access the latest updates and information. Android hacking can be done very well from computers running Mac or Linux but this book focuses on the PC user. You need an Android device if you wish to follow along with the examples and tutorial walkthroughs.

WHAT YOU NEED TO KNOW

1

ANDROID OS INTERNALS: UNDERSTANDING HOW YOUR DEVICE STARTS

IN THIS CHAPTER:

- The penguin down below: the Linux kernel
- Bootstrapping: How your device starts
- An introduction to custom bootloader and custom recovery processes

TO FULLY UNDERSTAND the process of rooting your device, gaining the control and power you need to truly customize it, you need to understand a little about how the Android operating system works—how the device goes from being powered off to a fully functioning state. It is in this process that developers usually exploit weaknesses to gain full access to the device. Usually some step in the boot process allows a developer to insert a bit of code or a script, and thus access functionality not intended by the Original Equipment Manufacturer (OEM).

Linux Development and Open Source

Linux began in 1991 with Linus Torvalds working to make a completely free and open source operating system that could be used by hobbyists, academia and hackers. His operating system has grown to be one of the most powerful and flexible in the world today. From a handful of unknown geeks, the developer base has matured to include thousands of contributors every year. Some of the finest names in computer science and programming work on the development not only of Linux but also of Android.

Linux remains completely free and completely open source. This allows companies and individuals to have access to the power of computing devices without the complex legal and copyright concerns that come with closed source software.

THE PENGUIN DOWN BELOW

Android is an operating system built on the Linux kernel. Thanks to Google and the Open Handset Alliance, Linux and its penguin mascot have found a home on Android devices. Android is essentially a highly customized distribution of Linux with various tweaks oriented towards mobile devices.

If you are familiar with the Linux operating system then you are going to feel quite at home with many aspects of the Android operating system. If you are comfortable with any other command-line operating system, such as DOS or the Windows command line, many of your skills there will be useful as well.

Android is, at its core, an implementation of the Linux operating system. Many of the commands you will be using in hacking an Android device are Linux commands. However, you do not need to be a programmer to become an Android hobbyist or enthusiast. Using the skills taught in this book, you can become adept at exploring and altering your Android device.

The differences between your Android device and a Linux desktop computer are many. The most striking difference is the way in which your device bootstraps (starts) when you power it on. It is in this start-up process that the hackers and elite developers find the vulnerabilities to exploit. Because Linux has a long history of being the go-to operating system of developers, hobbyists and hackers, there are many programmers and professional experts working on tools that help you with the root process. Most of the "heavy lifting" is done long before the average Android hacker gets access to root on his or her device.

Although you do not need to be a Linux nerd to root and customize your Android device, being familiar with the Linux command line, and command lines in general, will help you feel more comfortable. For an excellent reference to the Linux command line, check out *Linux Command Line and Shell Scripting Bible*, 2nd Edition by Richard Blum (Wiley, 2011).

HOW YOUR ANDROID DEVICE STARTS

The Android operating system has a complex and multistage start-up routine. Manufacturers lock the start-up process to protect revenue and maintain control of the device you purchase. The nature of the Android start-up process allows developers and hackers to replace parts of it to achieve full control of an Android device.

BOOTSTRAPPING

Bootstrapping (or booting) is a term that describes what a computing device does when turned on. It "pulls itself up by its bootstraps." When you power on an Android device, a tiny piece of code on a memory chip initializes the memory and CPU. Usually the bootstrap code is referred to as the boot-loader. The bootloader is different from device to device, although all bootloaders do the same things: they check for hardware features and load the first part of the operating system into the device's memory.

The encrypted bootloader is the beginning of all things Android, effectively locking out the user from customizing the firmware and software. Locking the bootloader is the rough equivalent to a computer manufacturer forcing you to use a particular version of Windows, along with a theme of their choosing. The bootloader is the primary point of contention between owners of mobile devices and the original equipment manufacturer (OEM). Many, if not most, OEMs specifically do not want you to have access to that boot-loader code. The reasons that OEMs do not want users to have access to this code are varied but fall into the following categories:

- **The cost of honoring warranties:** Altering the bootloader code can permanently disable the device. This is problematic for device manufacturers because broken devices are returned to them under warranty. It is difficult to determine if a device is broken because the user did something silly to it or if it is, in fact, defective. This means that the manufacturer may have to replace a device that became defective through no fault of the manufacturer. Replacing defective devices costs money and those costs may be passed on to the consumer.

- **The need to protect carrier agreements:** Carriers are paid to pre-install applications from third parties on devices. Many organizations, from car rental companies to streaming video startups, have a mobile application. To get exposure for their products, they pay carriers to include those applications on your device; to ensure that exposure, the carrier blocks the user's ability to remove the application. After all, it simply wouldn't do to have Blockbuster pay hundreds of thousands of dollars to have their application on your device only to have you remove it to make room for Angry Birds three minutes after you walk out of the store. Locking the bootloader allows carriers and OEMs to declare some applications as "system" applications. This removes them from typical management tasks, such as deletion or moving them to an SD card.

- **Planned obsolescence:** Devices with a very long life are bad for OEMs. The development and release cycle of new mobile devices has become incredibly fast, outpacing even old standards in technology. When a device is released, the device that will obsolete it is often already in production. Android operating system updates have new features and stability that users desire. Because OEMs depend on selling new features and the latest Android operating system, they need consumers to want the newest devices. Allowing consumers to update the operating system and software themselves effectively reduces the need to purchase the latest device from the OEM or carrier.

  In essence, planned obsolescence from the carriers and OEMs is designed to make the consumer spend more money to get the latest Android updates. If you can hack those updates into the perfectly good device you purchased six months earlier, the OEMs lose money.

When you power on an Android device, the bootloader is the first program code that runs. Bootloading is typically a two-part process, utilizing a primary and a secondary bootloader.

On most Android devices, the primary bootloader cannot be replaced. This is because the primary bootloader is hardcoded into an application-specific integrated circuit (ASIC) in the device. These hardcoded instructions load the secondary bootloader into memory and tell it where the memory, CPU and operating system are located and how they can be accessed.

Taking Responsibility for Your Hacks

It is important to note that if you choose to hack your device, you take responsibility for replacing it. It is unfair and unethical to do something silly to your device that disables it and then expect the carrier or OEM to replace it. Good hackers go into their hacks knowing the possible outcomes and willing to take responsibility for their own failures. When it comes to OEM and carrier ill-will towards hackers, ensure you are part of the solution not part of the problem. Never try to return a bricked or disabled device for replacement. Learn how to fix it or take responsibility and replace it.

ADDING A CUSTOM BOOTLOADER

A custom bootloader is a secondary bootloader that allows you to gain access to the file system with more control than you can with an OEM bootloader. Custom bootloaders open up the possibilities of replacing the original operating system files with customizations as varied as a new user interface or a supercharged kernel. Despite the manufacturer's objections, the hacker's goal is to interrupt the standard bootloading process and use a custom bootloader that enables hacking of the device.

UNDERSTANDING THE BOOTLOADER PROCESS

Your Android device follows certain steps when booting up. The following steps and Figure 1-1 are simplified and made generic to apply to most Android devices.

1. Special code in the boot read-only memory (ROM) locates the first-stage bootloader and loads it into memory. The boot ROM is an ASIC that has its code permanently programmed.

2. The first-stage bootloader loads the second-stage bootloader after initializing some memory and getting the hardware ready.

   The bootloader checks to see if the security flag is on (S-ON). If it is on, then the bootloader will load only signed (official) kernels. If the security flag is off (S-OFF), then the bootloader no longer checks for signatures. Setting S-OFF also releases other security lock downs, making the entire file system writable and enabling other goodies, such as allowing you to install a custom recovery process on the device.

   This is the step in which you want your custom bootloader to be loaded. The holy grail of hacking a manufacturer's handset is to load a custom bootloader so that a custom kernel can be loaded.

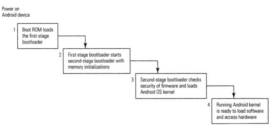

Figure 1-1: The Android boot process

Fastboot (see Chapter 3) is a protocol that allows low-level commands to be sent to a device to do such things as write files (such as custom bootloaders, recoveries and ROMs) to the operating system. Most manufacturers, therefore, disable the Fastboot protocol at the factory. Because the second-stage bootloader is the step in the boot process where the Fastboot protocol is enabled or disabled, this part of the code is frequently encrypted or otherwise locked down by OEMs. Some devices, such as Nexus devices and the Xoom, can be unlocked, allowing the Fastboot protocol to be enabled.

3. The bootloader loads a Linux kernel and customizations into memory. At this point, the bootloader hands off control of the hardware to the Linux kernel. The Linux kernel and any software or firmware customizations are usually all packaged together. On some devices, they are called a ROM. The name ROM is a slight misnomer because NAND storage is not truly read-only. Other devices require custom images (in IMG format) to be written to memory; still others have the kernel package written from an RUU file. However the kernel package is placed on the device, the bootloader must know where it is located and how to hand over the reins to it.

4. The last step is the initialization (INIT) process. The INIT process is the mother of all other processes that run on your device. It initializes all of the processes necessary for basic hardware access and device functionality. It also starts up the Dalvik virtual machine processes where most applications are executed.

Through this whole start-up process, the important thing for you to understand is that most of the hoops you have to jump through when rooting your Android are to achieve one or both of two goals:

- to set S-OFF, thereby allowing you to load your own custom kernel package
- to install a custom second-stage bootloader to allow you to ignore the S-ON or S-OFF state and load your own custom kernel package.

On some devices, neither goal is achievable and you must use workarounds to carry out device customizations. Devices with completely encrypted bootloaders, such as the Milestone and DroidX, can still be customized to some extent. The amount of customization you are able to achieve on these devices is limited and the process is usually a little more complex.

CUSTOM RECOVERIES: THE HOLY GRAIL

A recovery is a separate, standalone piece of code on a partition that can be booted in order to update Android and maintain the device. Almost all Android devices have a recovery mode into which they can be booted. One of your goals as an Android hacker is to get a custom recovery onto your device. Custom recoveries allow you to include many extra features, including easy customization and backup.

A recovery allows you to do useful things such as resetting a device to factory settings, clearing the data cache, and installing an official signed update to the Android operating system. Figure 1-2 shows the Amon Ra recovery screen. Unfortunately, the catch is that the default recovery process for most devices only installs updates to Android that have been signed with the OEM's digital signature.

If you can achieve full root and full custom recovery, you can easily change the ROM or firmware package installed on your Android device and create full file system backups, including backing up application data. Developers of custom recovery processes include many options not included in the standard Android boot process. Figure 1-3 shows the screen for the popular ClockworkMod recovery. This recovery gives you the capability of flashing a custom firmware package to your Android device very easily, as well as backing up the firmware, data, and cache and storing them on your SD card.

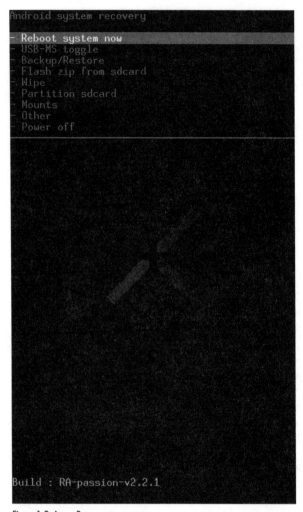

Figure 1-2: Amon Ra recovery screen

Which custom recovery you use depends on personal taste and the compatibility of your device. The Amon Ra and ClockworkMod recoveries each work on some devices. The XDA forums are a good resource to see if your device is supported by either of those custom recoveries. Typically, the process of rooting a device includes installing one of these recoveries. If your device is supported by a custom recovery, you should install it immediately after rooting. You can check the developer websites for device support.

Chapter 4 includes a complete walkthrough for the ClockworkMod recovery.

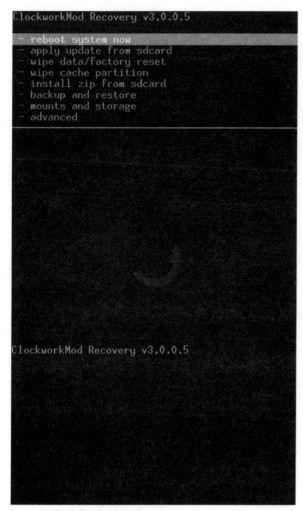

Figure 1-3: The ClockworkMod recovery screen

2

ROOTING YOUR ANDROID DEVICE

YOU HAVE PROBABLY heard your local Android geek mention rooting or read on the Web somewhere about rooting an Android device. Rooting may sound magical and mysterious, but it is a fairly simple idea. At its core, rooting gives the owner of a device more control and access.

The highest level of privilege you can have on a Linux system is to be logged into the device as the root user, sometimes called the superuser. The terms "superuser" and "root" both refer to the same thing.

Why Is It Called "Root"?

The term root comes from the hierarchical nature of the file system and permissions in UNIX and Linux operating systems. The branches of the file system and users resemble an inverted tree. The root of a file system is the beginning of all the files and directories. The root of the permissions system is the beginning of all permissions and, thereby, the most powerful and privileged.

The root level of permission exists on Linux systems to provide administrative access. Logged in as root, there is little that you cannot do. Root has permission to read and write most places in the file system and change system settings. Because of this, the highest goal for any hacker is to obtain the ability to log into a Linux device as root.

It is this very high level of privilege that you are seeking when you root an Android device. You need the root level of permission to customize your Android device in many ways.

WHY SHOULD YOU ROOT?

The benefits of rooting your device include saving money, as you extend the life and usefulness of your device, and fixing problems created during development or manufacture. There are also side benefits of adding functionality and removing restrictions imposed by the carrier or original equipment manufacturer (OEM). However, there are inherent risks in using root-level applications, as they are given access to all data from all applications installed on the device. Luckily, this risk can be mitigated by only giving root permissions to trusted applications.

INCREASING THE SERVICE LIFE OF THE DEVICE

One of my co-workers purchased one of the first Android devices released, the HTC Dream, also known as the G1. Matt loved the phone, but quickly realized that new versions of Android would run slowly or not at all on his device.

After the Éclair release of Android, it was simply not in the interest of the OEMs or the carriers to invest in recompiling Android for old hardware and working out all the bugs. Matt's G1 would eventually get the new version—but not soon enough. Carriers and OEMs would prefer you to purchase a new device with the latest Android version. However, developers in the Android and phone-hacking communities are determined to port new versions of Android to older devices to extend their lives with additional capabilities and features. Developers such as Koushik (Koush) Dutta and other teams working separately and in conjunction have ported new versions of Android to older hardware that OEMs and carriers have long since abandoned and stopped supporting. To install a newer version of Android on older hardware, you need to be rooted and have full file system access.

That original G1 purchased by Matt is still his everyday phone. Thanks to hackers at XDA and in the Android community, it sports the Froyo release of Android. The G1 was never supposed to have such a long life. Matt would have had to purchase at least two more devices after the G1 to access the manufacturer-supplied features of Android Froyo. Thanks to root access, Matt will be using his G1 for a while to come. (Yep, he is cool like that.)

FIXING OEM DEFECTS

As a result of the breakneck pace of mobile device development, far too many Android devices have shipped with some form of defect. Some of the defects are minor, such as dropping calls or writing slowly to the SD card. Other devices have shipped with major functional defects. For example, the Samsung Galaxy S device (known as the Fascinate when sold by Verizon and by other names when sold by other carriers) was designed with pretty curves that forced the GPS antenna into a bad position and caused the default GPS signal computation code to generate no or erroneous location data. An otherwise beautiful and powerful device was given an unnecessary and irritating, if not fatal, flaw.

The XDA forums and other Android hacking communities usually have a fix for design defects fairly quickly—even though it is difficult, if not impossible, to address a hardware defect with a software fix. However, installing a patch or fix frequently requires system write access, for which you need root permissions. Android users have come to expect that any defect or usage irritation can be fixed or patched by the Android hacker community. It has been said that even OEMs sometimes wait to see how the Android community fixes broken firmware before releasing their own patches.

Android Version Codenames

The initial release of Android had no name, but subsequent releases have all had a project name at Google. The first Android device to be popularly released was simply called the G1. It ran Android 1.5, known as Donut.

Someone at Google must have a sweet tooth because every version has been named after some sweet confection, starting with Donut. The subsequent versions have been called Éclair, Froyo, Gingerbread, and Honeycomb (the latter seems to bypass the sweet confections theme and cut straight to the sweet source). The latest version, Android 4.0, is called Ice Cream Sandwich.

INCREASING CAPABILITY

Many OEMs build devices with components that have capabilities they never intend to employ. For example, many Android devices have the capability to tune in to FM radio signals but that feature was never enabled and applications were not created for radio tuning. As a result of the work of the Android development community, the Nexus One gained both an FM radio and the ability to record in 720p resolution.

Overclocking

Almost every Android device has a CPU that can run at speeds faster than those enabled by the OEM. The CPUs are often clocked down to enhance battery life or reduce the possibility of heat issues. As distributed, the Xoom runs at 1 GHz, but it can be made to run safely and stably at 1.4 or 1.5 GHz. This gives an incredible performance boost to an already great device. Many other Android devices can have their CPU speed upgraded, giving faster performance and greater capability to the user. Speeding up the CPU is called overclocking and is a good reason to root your Android device.

Creating a Portable Hotspot

Many carriers produce devices that provide a wireless connection point (a "portable hotspot") to which you can connect, just as you would to any Wi-Fi hotspot. Such devices enable you to carry a hotspot around with you. A portable hotspot sends data over the cell network in the same way as your phone. There is little functional difference between your mobile device requesting Internet data and a portable hotspot requesting data from the Internet. Hotspots frequently cost as much as a smartphone and require an expensive data connection package in addition to what you already pay to access the same data on your Android device.

Rooting your Android device enables you to use your phone as a portable hotspot device. It is valuable to be able to create a temporary hotspot in an emergency or for a traveling business person to be able to do so regularly. Since you pay for data from your carrier, how you access that data should be your choice. Most OEMs disable this feature on your Android device unless you purchase an expensive hotspot package, and carriers have a vested interest in you purchasing more devices and more data plans. It's worth noting that, more often than not, using your phone as a hotspot violates the terms of service with your carrier, so tread carefully.

CUSTOMIZING THE DEVICE

Although perhaps not the most compelling factor, the desire to have complete power over the look and feel of your device is frequently the first reason for a hacker to want to root a device. Unless you have the power to write to any portion of the file system, your customizations will be temporary or limited in scope.

Once you have installed a custom recovery, you can write complete file system portions, including portions that are usually completely unchangeable. Installing customized firmware usually involves flashing a firmware or kernel package that includes user interface images and layouts, scripts, application packages, and much more. The time required to create these customizations would prevent most people from doing it. However, dedicated developers spend the long, geeky hours necessary to change the default firmware and release it as a ROM or other firmware package that enables rooted users to flash a large group of customizations all at once. Many developers release or announce new ROM packages on the XDA forums.

Overclocking a Device

Overclocking is a term that means "giving more speed." It comes from the technical idea that a computer's speed is based on "clock cycles" measured in hertz. Speeds of 500 MHz, 800 MHz and 1 GHz are measurements of how many clock cycles a processor goes through in a millisecond. Overclocking means forcing a chip to run at a clock speed that is higher than its native, or set, speed. This usually means increasing the voltage to the chip, which results in using more battery power, generating more heat and, most importantly, providing more speed to the device user.

The drawbacks of overclocking are that the increased heat and drop in battery life may reduce the life of the device. Manufacturers spend months perfecting the right frequency for the hardware based on the placement of chips, lifespan required, heat dissipation, and so on.

BACKING UP DATA

Most user data is safe from the destructive actions taken during rooting. However, applications and application data are removed by rooting or unlocking a device. For example, using the Fastboot OEM unlock described in Chapter 3 results in all of the /data partition being wiped. It is important to back up important data and assume that you will lose all data when hacking.

After you have succeeded in rooting your device, backing up the entire Android file system becomes very easy and provides great peace of mind when you change devices or customize a device. A rooted device can either perform a complete NANDroid backup, if it has a custom recovery, or a more finely tuned application-specific backup, using a program such as Titanium Backup.

CONTACT INFORMATION

Google keeps all of your Android phone and email contact information in its data cloud (that is, the information is stored on Google's servers). When you activate a phone with your login information, it pulls all of your stored contacts back to the phone. As long as you do not specifically create a contact that is stored only on the phone, Android devices automatically synchronize all contacts to the Google servers and you need never fear losing contact data.

Booting from an SD Card

Some Android devices, such as the Nook Color and WonderMedia tablets, require a custom SD card for rooting. A special file system and update script is written to an SD card using a PC. The SD card is then inserted into the device and the device is rebooted. The device boots from the SD card and flashes custom firmware and bootloaders.

If you find out from the XDA forum that your device needs to boot from an SD card, it is best to use a separate SD card on which you have not stored data. Most methods of making an SD card bootable will completely erase the data from it.

Often, rooting a phone or Android device sets the phone back to factory defaults, resulting in data (including contact information) being wiped from the phone. This means that you need to sign in to your Google account and let it synchronize all of your information. Many one-click root methods that run an exploit on your device will not wipe your data, though you should always be paranoid when it comes to backing up.

APPLICATIONS AND THEIR DATA

A similar situation exists when it comes to Google Apps Marketplace applications. When you download and install an application, a record that connects your login information with that application is stored on the Google servers. When you reactivate a device with your login information, it synchronizes automatically with the Google Apps Marketplace and automatically installs any missing applications.

> *Although applications are restored, any data stored by an application will most likely be lost unless it was specifically backed up or stored to the SD card. On some devices, you also risk losing all user-created data, such as photos and documents. If you have important data that has been created by an application, it's a good idea to find out how to back up and restore it (look on the XDA forum). It is best to assume that any hacking process will cause all your data to be wiped.*

DATA ON THE SD CARD

Android stores camera pictures and videos on your SD card, and you may want to back those up prior to hacking the device. Data stored on the SD card of an Android device is, typically, safe from rooting activities. However, it's always a good idea to use the Media Transport Protocol (for most Android 3.0+ devices—USB Mass Storage mode for others) or the ADB PULL command (see Chapter 3) to copy all of the data from your SD card to a backup folder on your computer.

HOW YOU CAN ROOT AND LEAVE YOUR OEM'S CONTROL

The process of rooting an Android device varies based on the model of your device. A device that has been available for a while may have multiple rooting methods. In the next section, we walk through the process of rooting with two devices. Chapters 3 and 4 cover most of the common skills and tools needed to obtain root.

The methods of obtaining root fall into broad categories:

- OEM flash software for writing firmware
- exploits
- native Fastboot flash
- scripted or automated methods.

These are very broad and subjective categories that I have created for organization of this section. Many developers will likely take me to task for the categorization of their method or utility.

You can find out what rooting methods are available by looking in the XDA forum for your specific device. For instance, the rooting information and procedures for my Xoom tablet are located in the Xoom Android Development subforum of the Motorola Xoom forum (`http://forum.xda-developers.com/forumdisplay.php?f=948`). Most proven root procedures are "stickied" at the top of the list of posts so that they are easy to locate.

Whether the bootloader or recovery is replaced on your device using flash software, an exploit or the Fastboot protocol, the principle is the same: root permission is the first step toward device customization.

OEM FLASH SOFTWARE

On some devices, the first time you acquire root, you must use the native OEM diagnostic or flash software. After flashing the firmware and accessing root, you will usually use a custom recovery for further firmware changes.

Educating Yourself

It is very important that you read everything that is available about your device. Read the initial root instructions and any stickied posts. Read the entire thread that is connected to your device's root procedure. Plan to spend a couple of days just reading up on other people's experiences with rooting, theming and ROMing your device. Most newbie mistakes are easily avoided if you take a long view and have enough patience to read everything available for and about your device. A hacker is a self-educated and very patient animal.

Because you are accepting all the risk and responsibility for destroying your device or making it better you should think more "marathon" than "sprint" when beginning in the rooting and hacking community. Read a lot and ask questions only after using the search function in the XDA forum.

In particular, it's a good idea to know your unbrick options (if there are any) before you attempt to root your device. In the XDA forum, search for the term "unbrick" and your device name.

Root can often only be achieved by flashing a complete signed firmware package with OEM tools. If your device requires an external program (other than the native Android SDK tools—Android Debug Bridge (ADB) and Fastboot) to write the new firmware the first time, then it will need a complete signed firmware package. For example, the first root method available for the Droid 1 involved using Motorola's RSDLite technician tool to flash a custom bootloader to the boot section of the file system. Similarly, many devices featuring the NVIDIA Tegra 2 processor require the use of NVFlash and Samsung devices often make use of ODIN.

Sometimes the only way to recover a bricked device is to use OEM flash software.

The advantages of using OEM flash software are that:

- It is usually fairly safe and straightforward to attempt.
- There are relatively few, uncomplicated steps in the process.

The disadvantages of using OEM flash software are that:

- It is sometimes difficult to use or understand. At best, the interface is sparse; at worse, it can be in language that you do not understand.
- OEM debugging software can be difficult to find and keep updated.

EXPLOITS

An exploit is a vulnerability (or "crack") in the operating system that can be exploited by a hacker. Exploits come in many types and formats. For instance, one of the earliest methods for gaining root on the EVO 4G was an exploit of a security vulnerability in the Adobe Flash application.

In the world of Linux operating systems, hacking through to a useable exploit is part science, part art and a lot of gut instinct built on experience. Finding a vulnerability that can be exploited is the first goal of the developer community when a new device is released. Advanced hackers and geeks race to be the ones to find the crack in the code that can be used to free a locked-down device. Threads exploring possibilities on the XDA forum can stretch to thousands of posts.

Exploits are some of the most fun and rewarding ways to root your Android device. About halfway through rooting my first HTC Thunderbolt using Scott Walker's ASH exploit, I remember thinking "Wow, I am really hacking this thing. I feel like an actor in *Mission Impossible*." That psneuter exploit written by Scott Walker (scotty2walker to the Android hacker community) is a good example of a simple exploit that was used to do some really cool stuff to get access to root. The psneuter script takes advantage of the fact that the Android Debug Bridge (see Chapter 3), if it cannot determine the S-ON/S-OFF state, assumes S-OFF and defaults to mounting the file system as readable and writable when you launch a remote shell access to an unrooted device. This little exploit can be utilized to write to sections of the file system, such as boot sections and recovery sections, that would other- wise be inaccessible.

I am not experienced enough and do not have the coding skills to program the psneuter exploit, but Scott Walker released the code to the Android community. As a result, I can use it to free my Android device. I have never had more fun than when participating with the Android community at the XDA forum to hack a new Android device.

The advantages of using an exploit are that:

- It can allow access to a tightly locked OEM device.
- It is fun and makes you feel like a hacker.
- It is usually difficult for the OEM to patch and eliminate the exploit.
- Anyone can do it using the skills outlined in this book.

The disadvantages of using an exploit are that:

- It is a complex process that requires knowledge and skill.
- It is easy to do something incorrectly.
- There is a high possibility of bricking the device.

NATIVE FASTBOOT FLASH

When a device is left unlocked or is unlockable, it can be booted into Fastboot protocol mode to accept Fastboot commands. Fastboot allows you to flash a complete file set or a file system bundled into a single file (known as an "image") to different areas of the file system, such as `boot` or `system`.

Most first-generation "Google experience" devices, such as the Nexus One, Xoom, and Nexus S, have unlockable bootloaders that allow the security switch (`S-OFF`) to be turned off, usually via the Fastboot command. However, not all devices support Fastboot natively. In other words, unless the OEM intended you to use Fastboot commands from your PC, you will not be able to do so. The Fastboot command and its capabilities are covered in Chapter 3.

The advantages of using Fastboot are that:

- The instructions are simple and fairly easy to follow.
- It is an easy method with relatively low risk.

The disadvantages of using Fastboot are that:

- A limited number of devices support it.
- Command-line skills are required.
- Performing a Fastboot OEM unlock will clear the `/data` partition on the device.

SCRIPTED AND ONE-CLICK METHODS

This is a very broad category that includes methods from the very sophisticated, such as the unRevoked root method, to simple ADB scripts. Scripted methods usually involve a lot less user interaction than step-by-step rooting methods that use ADB or OEM tools. As a result, they tend to be easier and more reliable. Custom binary methods, such as unRevoked, rely on a proprietary link across your USB connection or running an application directly on your device. Even so, proprietary methods perform the basic function of replacing the bootloader or recovery process on the file system.

Debate about Scripted and One-Click Roots

There is an ongoing debate in the Android community about one-click and scripted methods. Some developers fear that OEMs will crack down on these methods. Others argue that making rooting easier lowers the bar: the easier it is, the more people will accidentally brick their devices and attempt to replace them under warranty, causing OEMs to make rooting more difficult in their next release.

The clear advantage of using a scripted or one-click root method is that the process is much easier.

The disadvantages of using scripted and one-click methods are that:

- The hacker has less control over the process.
- The end result is achieved without long periods of frustration.
- Fewer devices are compatible with these methods.

ROOTING TWO DEVICES

This section provides a general overview comparing two methods of rooting at two levels of difficulty on two phones. The Nexus One is a developer's phone; it was designed to be very easy to root and customize, and we use Fastboot to root it. The Thunderbolt is more difficult to root, and we use the `psneuter` exploit script.

Don't worry about any terminology you do not understand. It will become more familiar to you as you proceed.

NEXUS ONE

In this section, we unlock and root a Nexus One phone. Google placed a removable lock on the bootloader, so first you have to unlock it using a developer tool called Fastboot. Once unlocked, the device is simple to hack and root. When an OEM allows community unlocking, it makes everything that follows simpler.

1. Connect the Nexus One phone to your computer with a USB cable.

2. Place the phone in Fastboot mode by booting while holding a combination of keys (the specific combination differs based on your device). Fastboot mode allows the phone to accept commands from the Fastboot protocol.

3. From a command shell window on your computer, run the following command to unlock the bootloader:

   ```
   fastboot OEM unlock
   ```

4. Reboot the phone once again into Fastboot mode.

5. Run a script to install the "superboot" bootloader on the device.

At this point, the Nexus One is completely rooted.

HTC THUNDERBOLT

A more difficult root is exemplified by the Thunderbolt from HTC. HTC locked the bootloader and made it very difficult to access the file system as a root user. This overview shows the increased level of complexity that comes with a locked bootloader. It is a high-level view of the steps necessary—see Chapter 9 for the down and dirty details.

1. Connect the Thunderbolt to your computer with a USB cable.

2. Use the ADB developer tool to push the following items to the SD card:
   - the `psneuter` exploit script
   - the BusyBox utility
   - a new bootloader image file.

3. Use ADB shell commands to change the permissions on the `psneuter` script and BusyBox so they can be executed.

4. Use ADB shell commands to run the `psneuter` exploit script to gain temporary root access to the system files.

5. Use the BusyBox MD5SUM command to make sure the image file is exactly the same as the original from which it was downloaded.

6. Use the BusyBox DD command to write the image file to the bootloader section of memory.

7. Use ADB shell commands to push a downgrade firmware signed by the OEM to the SD card.

8. Force the phone to reboot and install the signed downgrade firmware.

9. Use the ADB developer tool to push the following items to the SD card:

- the psneuter exploit script
- the BusyBox utility
- the wpthis script.

10. Set the permissions on psneuter and run it to gain ADB shell root access.

11. Set permissions on wpthis and run it to gain access to the locked bootloader.

12. Use ADB to push a new bootloader image to the SD card.

13. Write the new bootloader to the core first-level bootloader.

14. Use the BusyBox MD5SUM command to make sure the hash of the new bootloader matches the bootloader image file.

15. If the MD5SUM is incorrect, repeat Steps 12–14 until the MD5SUM is correct.

16. Push a new unsigned custom system firmware to the SD card.

17. Reboot the phone and let the new bootloader load the custom firmware.

At this point, the Thunderbolt has the S-OFF bootloader. There are then 10 more steps to install the SuperUser application and gain permanent root access. As you can see, rooting a device that has had its bootloader locked by the OEM is significantly more complex than rooting an unlocked device. Hacking a locked device to a free and open device is a rewarding experience that, once accomplished, will have you seeking to root more devices.

THE ROOT OF IT ALL

Once your device is rooted, it's really just the beginning. Applying custom firmware, known as a ROM, requires root access. If you want to remove OEM and carrier bloatware, you require root access.

AT&T previously prevented non-market applications being installed on devices it supplied. Rooting one of these devices allowed users to install non-market and custom applications on an otherwise severely limited phone.

Bloatware

As mentioned in Chapter 1, carriers and OEMs take money from service vendors or developers to place applications on your Android device. This helps them offset the cost of the device (or boost executive bonuses, depending on your point of view).

Whatever the reasons these applications are installed, they are permanent when your device is in its unrooted state. You cannot uninstall them or remove them. This is roughly analogous to purchasing a computer that can only have 19 programs installed on it and the manufacturer forces you to have 5 specific programs that you don't want to use. This bloatware occupies the very limited memory on your device and sometimes runs services you don't need or want, consuming battery and data storage.

Some low-budget tablets and phones cannot even install applications from the official Google Apps Marketplace. If you root such a device, you can install the Google Apps Marketplace and access all the goodies that more expensive devices can access.

As you can see, rooting your Android device is the doorway through which you can truly own your device. It eliminates carrier restrictions and removes the limitations that might otherwise force you to upgrade or purchase a different device.

3

THE RIGHT TOOL FOR THE JOB

MOST ROOT PROCEDURES rely on similar tools. The processes, exploits, and level of access may differ, but the toolkit you use to get a device to run with S-OFF or root file system access will always be fairly small. A solid understanding of the tools and how they are used will help you with your comfort level when rooting a new device.

READY, SET, . . . WAIT I HAVE TO HAVE WHAT?

Before starting most hacking jobs, or even an Android exploratory mission, you need to be able to connect your phone to your computer and you need access to hacking tools.

CONNECTING A PHONE TO A COMPUTER

You need to make sure that you have an appropriate cable for the physical connection to a PC and drivers to enable your computer to make sense of the connection. Many devices ship without drivers—they depend on native drivers included with the operating system installed on your computer.

Depending on the modes your device has when connected to a computer, the computer may recognize it as a mass-storage device and connect to it as if it were an external hard drive or memory card.

You need to install some form of debug or developer driver on your computer and make sure that USB Debugging (debug mode) is enabled for any interactions between the computer and the phone. Debug mode opens the connection with your computer and allows signals and commands to be sent to and received from Android.

HACKING TOOLS

Android hacking tools fall into three basic categories:

- developer tools from the SDK and third parties
- scripts
- Linux executables and commands on the phone.

Developer tools include the Android Debug Bridge (ADB) and more advanced tools, such as smali and baksmali, for taking apart Android application package (APK) files and putting them back together.

Some Linux shell commands are included on the Android device; others are placed on the device during the hacking process. The most popular and easiest bundle of Linux shell commands for Android is the BusyBox package (more on BusyBox later in this chapter). These commands are often executed in a script—a series of Linux shell commands that can be run either from the Android device or from an ADB shell on a connected computer.

Other Options

Some devices, such as the Nook Color and off-brand budget tablets, are hacked by creating a specially formatted SD card that contains custom firmware and scripts to be run by the Android device on boot. For those devices, the prerequisites are a little different. You usually need:

- a blank SD card
- a disk image file with the custom Android ROM and scripts
- an application on your computer to write raw disk images.

USB CABLES

Your device likely shipped with a cable to connect from the device to a computer. The most popular cable and connection type is the USB micro, shown in Figure 3-1.

Figure 3-1: A USB micro cable

Depending on how much and how roughly a cable has been used, it may be able to charge a phone or tablet but be completely unable to reliably transmit data. Some cheap cables (usually found with cheap car chargers) only have the charging pins of the micro USB jack connected, so they will never be able to connect to your computer for data transfer. If your OEM's cable is in great condition without harsh bends, kinks or cat tooth marks, then you should be fine. However, if you have lost, damaged or replaced your OEM cable make sure that you replace it with a similar cable.

A USB cable is a USB cable. However, not all USB cables are created equally in terms of quality and fit. The micro jack end of a USB cable is particularly prone to have a poor fit that gives a bad connection or poorly supports the delicate jack socket components. Unfortunately, USB cable issues can be difficult to diagnose or detect. Unless you have disconnection issues that are obviously related to movement, you will need to have a spare cable to swap with a suspected bad cable.

> *If you connect your device via a USB hub or a USB port on the front of your computer, you are likely to experience connection issues. Your device should be connected to a USB port on the back of your computer or one you know is directly connected to the main USB bus.*
>
> *I struggled for hours with my Xoom USB cable plugged into a front USB port. The device connects but appears as "offline". It instantly connects "online" when I plug the USB cable into the rear of my computer.*

USB DEBUGGING

With a known, or assumed, good USB cable connection, you need to turn on USB debugging on your phone or tablet. Debug mode allows ADB system commands to travel between your device and your computer. You can also view system logs and the file structure, and push or pull applications and files. However, some caution must be exercised when enabling USB debugging, as a connected computer can potentially install applications, copy data, and read logs on the device.

It is important to remember that many operations you perform while in debug mode end by automatically resetting or turning off USB debugging. This means that before each major step in a hacking procedure you need to check that your device is in debug mode. Luckily Android makes this very easy. Whenever your device is in debug mode, you will see the debug mode icon in the notification bar (see Figure 3-2).

If you don't see the debug icon, you do not have debug connectivity and ADB will not work. On most Android devices, the following steps turn on USB debugging:

1. Access the device settings, usually by tapping the Menu key or soft button on the home screen. (On the Xoom and some other tablet devices, you must tap the area near the clock and then tap Settings.)

2. On the Settings menu, tap Applications.

3. Tap Development.

4. Tap the USB debugging check box.

5. Click OK on the notification.

The debugging icon should be visible in the notifications area as in Figure 3-2.

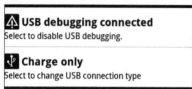

Figure 3-2: Debug mode notifications from the Nexus One (top) and the EVO 3D (bottom)

Some Android devices have the ability to put the USB port into other modes, such as "charge only" or "mass storage". You may need to experiment to determine which USB port settings allow your device to work with ADB. Usually the "charge only" or "Sync" settings allow you to start hacking across the ADB connection. Check the XDA forum for your device—it is likely that someone has already figured out the required settings for you to connect cleanly.

WHAT'S DRIVING THIS THING?

The first time you connect your device, a default set of operating system drivers are likely to be used. These drivers are likely to be good enough for SD card access and charging. However, ADB needs specific kinds of connectivity that usually requires developer or OEM drivers. The next section shows you how to verify that you have the correct connectivity.

To verify the driver that you have installed on your computer, you will want to see that there is a driver with "ADB" or "Debug Driver" in the description. The steps are different for different operating systems. On Windows, use the Device Manager to look for an item that refers to your device OEM's name.

In other words, if your device is manufactured by Motorola, you are looking for a device with "Motorola" or something similar in the name. If you see an item with ADB in the device name, the correct drivers are installed. However, if there is a warning or error icon (an exclamation point or red X), the correct device driver may not be installed or the connection may be malfunctioning.

To locate the correct drivers for your device, you usually need to download them from your OEM's support website. It is not always easy to locate the correct device packages even when you know what you are looking for. The XDA device forums frequently have a "sticky" post that contains links to device driver downloads. Some OEMs, such as Motorola, have a device driver helper that scans for connected devices and downloads the correct drivers.

USING THE ANDROID DEBUG BRIDGE

In this section, we demystify the Android Debug Bridge and walk through all of the commands you need to start freeform hacking or to follow rooting instructions. The Android Debug Bridge (usually called ADB) allows you to connect your Android device to your computer.

ADB is a command-line tool that runs with various switches or parameters to do different tasks. In today's world of pretty point-and-click interfaces, returning to a command-line interface may seem counterintuitive, though any good hacker worth his weight in unlocked cell phones is comfortable using a command line.

The commands with which you need to be familiar can be broadly separated into two categories:

- Commands that do something **to** the Android device. These commands start with one of the Android SDK commands, such as `adb` or `fastboot`.
- Commands that do something **on** or **in** the Android device. These commands are run in the Android shell and are usually entered on a command line that starts with a hash symbol (#) or a dollar sign ($).

Some of the commands you will use are not ADB or Android commands but commands for your computer's operating system. The most common operating system commands you may need are:

- **change directory:** to change the command prompt context to a different folder (`cd` on Windows, Mac and Linux)
- **directory listing:** to list the files and folders in the current folder (`dir` on Windows; `ls` on Mac and Linux)
- **make directory:** to make a subfolder in the current folder (`mkdir` on Windows, Mac and Linux).

Connectivity between your device and your computer is the starting point for all hacking. Familiarity with ADB and its basic commands will help you as you follow more detailed rooting or hacking instructions. I have found that a fear of, or unfamiliarity with, ADB is the primary stumbling block for beginner hackers. If you use each of the commands once during this walkthrough, you will be set to follow actual hacking walkthroughs.

None of the following examples and walkthroughs make harmful changes to your device. However, if you want to play it very safe (like a really good hacker), make sure you back up any data from your device's SD card. You must select the appropriate option in your device's Privacy Settings menu to enable backing up and restoring of your data and applications.

Contacts and applications you have downloaded from the Google Apps Marketplace are stored in the Google cloud and will restore themselves if necessary.

The rest of this chapter assumes you have the Android SDK tools installed on your computer. Refer to Appendix A for the SDK setup procedure if you get the message shown in Figure 3-3.

Figure 3-3: Message indicating that the Android SDK is not set up or not in the current folder

CHECKING DEVICE CONNECTIVITY

This section describes the most effective way to determine if your computer has the right amount and correct kind of connectivity with your computer.

The adb devices command allows you to see the devices connected to your computer in the Android debug context. It is also the command most Android developers will ask you to run at the beginning of any troubleshooting steps.

Make sure that your Android device is connected to your computer and you have the drivers installed before continuing. Refer to the appropriate XDA forum for links to device drivers you may need.

1. Open a command prompt window. (In Windows, press Windows+R; type cmd in the Run dialog box and press Enter.)

2. Type adb devices.

   The results should be as shown in Figure 3-4 if your device is connected and the correct drivers are installed. If no device serial number is listed, then ADB is working correctly but your device is not connected or the driver isn't installed (see the "Troubleshooting a Connection" sidebar).

Figure 3-4: The adb devices command showing a connected HTC device

If you get the response shown in Figure 3-3, then the ADB folder is probably not set up correctly in your PATH variable. Refer to Appendix A for setting up ADB so that it is accessible from any folder.

If everything is correctly connected, the adb devices command returns a list of devices connected to the computer. If you have more than one connected Android device in debug mode, each is listed with its serial number. Any Android emulators you may have running also show up.

You can specify the device to which you want to send an ADB command by giving its serial number. This is very tedious and it is easier to connect only the device with which you are currently working.

RESTARTING THE ADB SERVICE

Restart the ADB service from the command prompt with the following steps:

1. Type adb kill-server and press Enter.

2. Type adb start-server and press Enter.

This shuts down the ADB service gracefully and re-initializes it. You can then check again for device connectivity using adb devices.

Troubleshooting a Connection

Sometimes your device will lose its connection. When this happens, the `adb devices` command returns "List of connected devices" followed by the word "offline". This means that ADB knows there is a device connected but it cannot communicate with the device.

Use the mnemonic DUCK to remind you of the steps to take in troubleshooting a connection:

- ◆ Debug mode: Make sure the device is in debug mode.
- ◆ USB: Make sure the USB cable is connected to an appropriate (rear) port and that the Android device is in the proper USB mode.
- ◆ Context: Make sure you are running your ADB command from a folder in which the ADB binary executable is accessible.
- ◆ Kill: If the connection still does not function, you may have to kill and restart the ADB server.

You may have to reboot both the computer and the Android device. You should verify that the driver is correctly installed and reinstall if necessary.

You should also check the XDA forum for common or known connection issues with your device.

COPYING FILES TO AND FROM YOUR DEVICE

One of the most useful things you can be comfortable doing is "pushing" files to and "pulling" files from your device. Most root and `S-OFF` hacks require pushing a script to a device and then running it locally on the device. This walkthrough has you push a simple text file to your SD card and look on your device to see that it is located there. Doing this once with an innocuous text file will give you the comfort level you need to push other types of file to your device.

> *Make sure you have a local file system explorer on your device, such as RootExplorer or ES File Explorer. You need to be able to explore the device file system to verify that pushing a file to your phone has worked.*

First, you need to create a text file:

1. Open a command prompt window and note the path.
2. Use Windows Explorer to navigate to that folder.

3. Right-click in Windows Explorer and select New → Text File.

4. Rename the text file to `sample.txt`.

The `adb push` command uses the following pattern:

```
adb push <desired local file> <desired target location>
```

Copy the text file to the device. Switch back to the command prompt window and enter the following command:

```
adb push sample.txt /sdcard/sample.txt
```

The response should be similar to Figure 3-5.

Figure 3-5: The results of the adb push command sequence

If the file you want to push to the device is not in the current context folder, you need to use its full path, as shown in Figure 3-6.

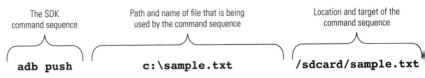

Figure 3-6: The syntax of the adb push command sequence

If `adb push` *returns an error message saying that the file system is "read only", restart the ADB server and attempt the activities again. If you still have problems, try replacing the path to the SD card with the path to the* `tmp` *file area (*`/data/local/tmp`*) to which you may have more access on an unrooted device.*

Now let's check the SD card on your device to see the pushed file. Open the file explorer on the device. Navigate to the root of your SD card. Depending on the file explorer, it may be the default folder; if not, it will be a folder listed in the root of the file system. Figure 3-7 shows the file on the SD card using ES File Explorer.

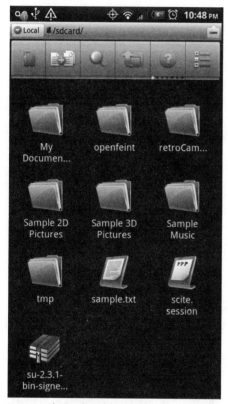

Figure 3-7: The sample.txt file on the SD card in ES File Explorer

Now you are going to pull the file from the device back to your computer. The adb pull command uses the following pattern:

```
adb pull <desired device file> <desired local file>
```

The command syntax is similar to that shown in Figure 3-6, with pull instead of push.

In your command prompt window, enter the following command:

```
adb pull /sdcard/sample.txt sample2.txt
```

Remember to press the Enter key after you enter the command.

Now type `dir *.txt` and then press the Enter key. This will give you a list of all the `.txt` files in the current folder. You should see the `sample2.txt` file that has been pulled from your Android device.

> *The pull command pulled a file named `sample.txt` and wrote it to your local file system under the new name `sample2.txt`. You will see this again in the section about file management and will do it many times when following a root instruction guide from the XDA forum. Pulling a file to a new name allows you to keep copies of the file straight and is sometimes necessary to correctly flash image files or updates.*

You may often want to back up some part of your Android device's file system to your computer. You may want to pull a specific application or system file, alter it on your local computer and then push it back to your Android device. You can copy any file using the `adb pull` and `adb push` commands.

REBOOTING A DEVICE

After flashing an image or writing a file to the file system, it is sometimes necessary to reboot the device cleanly. The `adb reboot` command allows you to reboot your Android device from the command line of your computer. You can use the `adb reboot` command with one of two switches:

- **bootloader:** This option boots the device into the bootloader menu (as shown in Figure 3-8). The bootloader menu is sometimes used to access Fastboot and to flash official firmware updates. From the bootloader menu, you can boot the bootloader sequence, reboot the device or power down the device.
- **recovery:** This option boots the device into the recovery installed on the device. It reboots into the firmware (the factory recovery or a custom recovery) installed in the recovery partition.

Figure 3-8: The Bootloader screen of the Motorola XOOM after running adb reboot bootloader

THE POWER OF FASTBOOT

The Fastboot command from the Android SDK is a powerful tool for writing to the file system partitions of an Android device. You will mostly use Fastboot commands to flash image files and the contained file systems to various partitions such as the system, boot and recovery partitions.

Fastboot commands are not so much exploratory or hacking tools as they are specific tools used when you are going to fundamentally change the file system on an Android device. As such, you should only use them when you know specifically what you are trying to accomplish. Not all devices can boot to Fastboot mode. Typically, you only use Fastboot commands on devices that have the ability to unlock the bootloader.

The Fastboot command does not live in the same folder as the `adb` command. Fastboot is in the `C:\Program Files (x86)\Android\ android-sdk-windows\tools\` folder.

As with the `adb` command, you use various commands and options following `fastboot` to change what the Fastboot command does. The walkthroughs and activities below require that your phone be in Fastboot mode. Follow the steps below to attempt to put your device in Fastboot mode:

1. Connect your device to your computer and verify connectivity using `adb devices`.

2. Type `adb reboot bootloader` and press Enter.

Your device should reboot into the bootloader. Make sure to select "FAST-BOOT" or equivalent from the bootloader menu (see Figure 3-8).

UNLOCKING A DEVICE

A few devices, such as the Nexus One and Xoom tablets, have a built-in ability to unlock and allow the following command to be run:

```
fastboot OEM unlock
```

This command sequence unlocks the bootloader and allows you to run Fastboot flash and other commands so that root can be acquired.

UPDATING A DEVICE

The following command flashes an `update.zip` file to the Android device:

```
fastboot update
```

This command is not used much in hacking or rooting procedures although it can be used to bring back a device that is softbricked. If the device can receive Fastboot commands and you have a full file system in an `update.zip` file, you can restore the device from that file.

FLASHING A DEVICE

The flash command is perhaps the most useful Fastboot command. It allows you to write the contents of an image file to a named partition on your Android device. The argument to the command names the partition that is to be flashed:

```
fastboot flash boot
fastboot flash system
fastboot flash recovery
```

On devices that have been unlocked, the flash command is frequently used to flash a file system with root access. For example, if you have a new `boot.img` file that contains an unlocked bootloader or root access permissions, you can use the flash command to write the contents to the boot partition.

It is important to note that flashing the wrong thing or interrupting the flashing process can permanently brick your device. Never flash an image file to a partition unless you are certain that you have the correct file for your device and you have read up on the process in the appropriate XDA forum.

REBOOTING A DEVICE

This command is sometimes used after the Fastboot flash command to reboot the device so that the flashed file system can be booted:

```
fastboot reboot
```

Instead of booting normally, the following command boots your Android device directly into the bootloader:

```
fastboot reboot-bootloader
```

HARNESSING THE POWER OF THE PENGUIN WITH ADB SHELL

ADB can also be used as a direct connection to the Android operating system and harness the power of Linux. The commands that can be run from inside the operating system shell are many and varied.

> The adb shell *command opens up your Android device to allow you to run commands directly on the device. The shell is frequently utilized to make changes to the base Android operating system files.*

When you connect to an Android device using ADB shell, the command prompt on your computer changes to indicate you are no longer entering commands that are being picked up and interpreted by your local computer. Instead you are in the Android operating system and the commands you enter at the prompt are picked up and interpreted by it.

To load the shell, type the command adb shell. The familiar command prompt changes to an enigmatic $ or #. The dollar sign ($) is the Android operating system's way of telling you that it is waiting for input but that you are not a "privileged" user so you can't really harm anything by poking around. You only see the hashtag (#) prompt if you are in the Android operating system as root user. The hashtag is a beautiful thing to the Android hacker: it means that you have ultimate control over the Android file system.

While in the ADB shell, you need to enter Linux (not DOS) commands. For instance, to get a listing of files and folders in a folder, you enter the command ls instead of dir.

You can send shell commands to your Android device without starting the interactive shell. For example, if you enter the following command:

```
adb shell cp /sdcard/sample.txt
  /sdcard/sample2.txt
```

it is performed as if it had been entered on the command line of the shell. Many rooting instructions have you run ADB shell commands in this way. It is a shortcut that allows interactive commands to be run without actually being in the Android shell.

FILE SYSTEM NAVIGATION

In this example, you open the ADB shell and use a few Linux commands to navigate the file system. The commands we cover here are included in the default Android configuration. Because Android is a slimmed down and customized version of Linux, it only uses a very small subset of the possible Linux commands. A later section deals with the more complex Linux commands that you install with the excellent BusyBox package.

In this section, we open an ADB shell prompt, navigate through the file system and exit from the file system.

Accessing the ADB Shell Prompt

Follow these steps to open an ADB shell prompt:

1. Open a command prompt window on your local computer.
2. Enter the command `adb shell`.

If your ADB environment has been set up correctly, you are in the Android shell. If you receive an error message, check for connectivity (remember the DUCK troubleshooting model).

If your phone is currently unrooted, you should see the prompt change to a dollar sign ($) followed by a flashing cursor (see Figure 3-9).

Your command prompt window is no longer operating in the context of your local computer. Instead it is a "shell" that is mirroring directly to the Android operating system.

Figure 3-9: The ADB shell in the Android operating system

Listing the Files in a Folder

Now take a look at the files and folders in your current Android folder. Type the command ls followed by the Enter key. (Remember, commands are not executed until you press the Enter key.)

Look at the listed files and folders. It is not readily apparent which are folders and which are files. Unless you add flags to the ls command, Linux (and, therefore, Android) does not make any visual distinction between files and folders. Poking around in Android sometimes means typing a more advanced version of the list command to see what kind of file is in a particular folder listing.

> *Any time you see a file or folder with the name preceded by a period, it is a hidden file or folder. At this point, you are not likely to see hidden files or folders. The command ls -s allows you to see these less obvious files.*

Navigating the File System

The next activity walks you through the important skills of viewing your current folder contents and navigating from folder to folder.

1. In the ADB shell window, type the following command to go to the root of the file system: cd /.

2. Enter the command ls. Now you should see files such as system and etc in the folder listing.

3. Enter the command cd system to change your active folder context to the system folder.

4. Type the command `ls`. You should see the files and folders that are located in the `system` folder scroll past.

5. Now navigate back to the root of your file system by using the command `cd /`.

> *Linux, and thus Android, is a case-sensitive operating system. So the command `cd System` returns an error. It is important to keep this case sensitivity in mind as you begin hacking in Android. Remember that CASE MATTERS!*

Using the `cd` command, you can wander all through your Android file system. Using the `ls` command, you can see the folders and files in the current folder.

It will help if you keep in mind that the Android file system is like an inverted tree (see Figure 3-10), with the other folders branching down from the root folder. Using the `cd` command to navigate into a parent folder takes you up in the hierarchy.

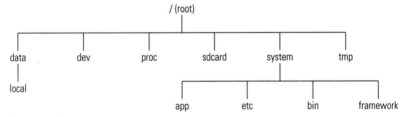

Figure 3-10: The Android file system "tree"

You can use the following shortcut command to navigate up one level in the folder hierarchy:

```
cd ..
```

If you start at root and navigate to `/sdcard` and then to `/myfolder`, your full path is `/sdcard/myfolder`. Entering the command `cd ..` then moves back up from your current location to `/sdcard`.

FILE MANAGEMENT

Hacking is all about getting access and permissions that are not standard. So you need three basic skills for hacking:

- navigating and managing files
- determining who has what kind of access to files
- changing who has what kind of access to a file.

We have covered navigation and now we go on to learn how to manipulate files and the access to them.

In the process of hacking certain devices, you will need to move files to and from the SD card. The SD card is a low-privilege file system, which means that you can place files on the SD card and then pull them into the primary file system, usually after exploiting some part of the system with a script such as psneuter.

> *Some file management tools are not available until you follow the steps to install BusyBox on a rooted device. We discuss BusyBox at the end of this chapter and in the device walkthroughs.*

Copying Files

The first thing you need to do is be able to copy files from one location to another. In any Linux-based operating system, you use the cp command to copy files or folders from one location to another. The cp command uses the pattern:

```
cp <source file name> <destination file name>
```

For example, the command cp sample.txt sample2.txt takes the sample.txt file and copies it to a new file named sample2.txt. So there would then be two files: sample.txt and sample2.txt.

The cp command can also take full path names to copy one file to another location. To copy a file to new location, specify the full path for the destination:

```
cp sample.txt /sdcard/my_folder/sample2.txt
```

Frequently, you will use adb push to put an exploit script or firmware file onto your SD card and then use cp to move and rename it.

Deleting Files

The remove (rm) command allows you to delete files and folders from the file system. The remove command uses the pattern:

```
rm <path and file name>
```

There is no recycle bin in Android, so the results of this command are not reversible.

Moving Files

The move command is equivalent to copying a file and deleting the original. When BusyBox (covered later this chapter) is installed on a rooted device, the move command is available.

```
mv sample.txt /sdcard/sample2.txt
```

The above command copies the `sample.txt` file to a new file on the SD card named `sample2.txt` and then removes `sample.txt` from the current folder.

File Management Walkthrough

If you still have the `sample.txt` file from the "Copying Files to and from Your Device" section on your SD card, you can now use file management commands to play around with it. If you do not have the file on your SD card, push a `sample.txt` file to your SD card.

1. Start ADB shell by running `adb shell` from the command prompt window.
2. At the $ prompt, enter the command `cd \sdcard`.
3. Enter the command `ls -l`.
4. Verify that the file `sample.txt` is listed.
5. Enter the command `cp sample.txt samplecopy.txt`.

Now let's make a new folder and copy the `samplecopy.txt` file to it.

1. Enter the following command: `mkdir MyDirectory`.
2. Enter the following command:

```
cp samplecopy.txt /MyDirectory/samplecopy2.txt
```

> *Filenames and commands in Linux and Android are case sensitive, so* `mydirectory` *is an entirely different name from* `MyDirectory`.

Now delete the old copy of `samplecopy.txt` and verify the file was moved to `MyDirectory`.

1. Enter the command: `rm samplecopy.txt`.
2. Enter the command `ls -l` and check that `samplecopy.txt` is not there.
3. Enter the command `cd MyDirectory`.
4. Enter the command `ls -l` and check that `samplecopy.txt` is there.

FILE ACCESS PERMISSIONS

Many commands in the Android shell can take "switches." A switch is a parameter that is entered with the command to change the way the command does its job. Let's look at the switches for the list (`ls`) command you learned earlier. In the ADB shell, type the following command:

```
ls -?
```

The shell throws an error but then shows you all the acceptable switches for the `ls` command. If you use any unacceptable syntax with a command, it shows you a quick listing of the accepted switches and parameters. In a full Linux installation, you would be able to use the `man` command to see the appropriate manual page. Android is a trimmed-down version of Linux and does not include the manual pages for common commands.

Seeing File Access Permissions

Notice that one of the switches that you can use with `ls` is the `-l` (that's a lowercase L, not a numeric 1) switch. When you use this switch, the `ls` command shows much more information. Let's try it. Type the following command in your ADB shell:

```
ls -l
```

Your output should resemble Figure 3-11. Notice all the gibberish at the start of each line—lots of Ds, Rs, Ws and Xs.

```
C:\Users\Administrator>adb shell
# ls -l
ls -l
drwxr-xr-x    3 root     root            0 Jan 30 11:31 acct
drwxrwx--x    1 system   cache        2048 Jan 30 01:22 cache
dr-x------    2 root     root            0 Jan 30 11:31 config
lrwxrwxrwx    1 root     root           17 Jan 30 11:31 d -> /sys/kernel/debug
drwxrwx--x    1 system   system       2048 Jan 30 01:22 data
-rw-r--r--    1 root     root          118 Dec 31  1969 default.prop
drwxr-xr-x   12 root     root         1280 Jan 30 11:31 dev
lrwxrwxrwx    1 root     root           11 Jan 30 11:31 etc -> /system/etc
-rwxr-x---    1 root     root        94360 Jan 30 11:31 init
-rwxr-x---    1 root     root         1677 Dec 31  1969 init.goldfish.rc
-rwxr-x---    1 root     root         3464 Dec 31  1969 init.mahimahi.rc
-rwxr-x---    1 root     root        15021 Dec 31  1969 init.rc
drwxrwxr-x    6 root     system          0 Jan 30 11:31 mnt
dr-xr-xr-x  100 root     root            0 Dec 31  1969 proc
drwx------    2 root     root            0 Apr  6  2011 root
drwxr-x---    2 root     root            0 Dec 31  1969 sbin
drwxrwx--x    2 system   system          0 Jan 30 11:31 sd-ext
lrwxrwxrwx    1 root     root           11 Jan 30 11:31 sdcard -> /mnt/sdcard
drwxr-xr-x   16 root     root            0 Jan 30 11:31 sys
drwxr-xr-x    1 root     root         2048 Jan 30 01:21 system
-rw-r--r--    1 root     root            0 Dec 31  1969 ueventd.goldfish.rc
-rw-r--r--    1 root     root           26 Dec 31  1969 ueventd.mahimahi.rc
-rw-r--r--    1 root     root         3908 Dec 31  1969 ueventd.rc
lrwxrwxrwx    1 root     root           14 Jan 30 11:31 vendor -> /system/vendo
r
#
```

Figure 3-11: Output from ls -l

You can consider the leftmost column of information in Figure 3-11 to be a table of rows and columns. Each row refers to the file on the right and the columns contain information about that file (see Table 3-1). Column 1 indicates a folder by the letter "d." The next nine columns refer to the access permissions for a class of person. Columns 2–4 show the access permissions for the User class; columns 5–7 for the Group class; and columns 8–10 for the Others class.

Table 3-1   File information

Purpose	Folder	User			Group			Others		
Column	1	2	3	4	5	6	7	8	9	10
Value	d	r	w	x	r	w	-	r	w	-

The two aspects of permissions on an Android file are who has the permission and what kind of permission they have. The who definition is broken down into three classes of people:

- **User** is the owner of the file.
- **Group** means all the users who are in the same group as the file's owner.
- **Others** means all the other users on the device.

Each group of three columns records the kinds of permission (Read, Write and eXecute) that the class of people have on the file. Table 3.1 shows the possible value of each column. If a class does not have a particular permission, there is a dash in that column.

> *On an Android device, the important permission columns are those for User and Others. You will need to change the permission levels of some scripts and binary files you add to an unhacked device.*

Changing File Access Permissions

The change mode command (chmod) is one of the single most important commands you can learn in Android hacking. It is the command that changes the permissions and access to files and folders.

You can set the permission level for a certain class using U, G and O to indicate User, Group and Others and using an operator (+ or -) to add or remove a permission. For example, the following command would set the read and execute permissions for the User and Others classes:

```
chmod uo + rx <file name>
```

Now that may seem simple enough but instructions and walkthroughs usually don't use chmod in that way. Instead, they use a numeric value for a particular level of permission for each class. The possible numeric values and their meanings are listed in Table 3-2.

Table 3-2   Options for the chmod command

Value	Permission
7	Full
6	Read and write
5	Read and execute
4	Read only
3	Write and execute
2	Write only
1	Execute only
0	None

A single numeric value represents the permission for each of the three classes of user or group. If you determine that your sample.txt file should give full rights to User and read-only access to the Group and Others classes, then that permission could be set using the following command:

```
chmod 0744 sample.txt
```

> If you do not have root access, you may not be able to carry out the following activity on files in your SD card folder. If this is the case, push the sample.txt file to the /data/local/tmp folder on your device and then try the activity again.

1. In your ADB shell window, enter the command cd /sdcard.
2. Enter the command ls to verify that sample.txt is still there.
3. Enter the command ls -l sample.txt to see which permission levels are set for the file.

4. Enter the command `chmod 0775 sample.txt` to make `sample.txt` executable.

5. Enter the command `chmod 0766 sample.txt` to change the permissions for Group and Others to read and write only.

At first, the `chmod` command can seem very daunting and confusing. Usually you do not need to worry about the overall structure of permissions for files and folders; the instructions for a rooting procedure simply tell you which file to change permissions on and how to do it.

REDIRECTION AND PIPING

Redirection allows you to write the output of a command to disk. The redirection operator (>) causes the output of a command to be written to a named file (if the file already exists, it is overwritten). For example, the following command puts the list of files into `listing.txt`:

```
ls -l > listing.txt
```

Piping means using the output of one command as the input of another command. The pipe operator (|) takes the output of a command and sends it as input to another command. For example, the following command takes the folder listing and pipes it to the `more` command (which displays the output one screen at a time and prompts the user for the next screen):

```
ls -l | more
```

1. In your ADB shell window, enter the command `ls -l > \sdcard\ listing.txt`.

2. Enter the command `more \sdcard\listing.txt` to display the contents of the `listing.txt` file created with the redirection symbol.

3. Enter the command `ls -l | more` to see that the pipe gives the same result as Steps 1 and 2.

CONCATENATION

The concatenate command (`cat`) takes the content of a file or file structure and streams it out to a file or to the screen. For example, you can stream the contents of a file system to a single file using the redirection operator. For instance to get a bit by bit copy of a file system, you could use the following command:

```
cat /data  >data.img
```

This command outputs the contents of the `/data` folder to an image file.

BUSYBOX: GIVING THE PENGUIN BACK ITS POWER

Only a handful of Linux operating system commands are included with Android. BusyBox is an excellent multi-utility binary that was originally developed by Bruce Perens and has matured into an incredible Swiss Army knife of Linux utilities. It is currently maintained by Stericson, a senior moderator at XDA. When you install the BusyBox binary, you get a much larger subset of Linux commands, all optimized for small systems and limited resources. Because the BusyBox utilities are in a single binary, they can share code, which makes for a small installation package.

BusyBox will be a constant companion in your hacking of Android devices. A lot of the advanced Linux tools you require are not available until BusyBox is installed. For this reason, installing BusyBox is frequently one of your first tasks in a rooting or hacking session. The process of installing and linking the BusyBox commands differs between devices. Rooting instructions usually have installing BusyBox as a step. Search the XDA forums for instructions on installing BusyBox on your device.

Some applications that require root may also require that BusyBox is installed as they may depend on some of the commands in BusyBox.

Over 200 commands can be compiled into BusyBox. In the course of hacking, you will probably use only a fraction of them. Here we cover three of the most frequently used commands from the awesome BusyBox binary. They are used from your Android command shell or an Android terminal program.

THE DD COMMAND

The dd command is a specialized command that uses low-level bit copying to copy and convert data from a source to a given destination. In Android hacking, dd is frequently used to write an image file to a memory location or file location when the data and result must be exact, so that it can be verified and used for critical processes such as operating system boot files.

The dd command uses the following syntax:

```
dd if=<source file> of=<target file>
```

- The if (input file) parameter tells the command where to find the source file.
- The of (output file) parameter tells the command where to write the target file.

You should take special care with the parameters: reversing the if
and of *parameters would be catastrophic.*

THE ECHO COMMAND

The echo command simply writes a string to the screen (known as stdout
in Linux). In Android hacking, it is sometimes used to trick the system into
believing it has received a specialized system message such as "Hey, there is
an update available on the SD card—you should install it."

THE MD5SUM COMMAND

The md5sum command allows you to hash a file using the MD5 algorithm
and see the output. This is a very accurate and easy way to see if files in
different locations are the same. When someone has used the md5sum
command to hash a file, they publish the short hash string and you can
compare it to the hash you create locally. If two hash strings match, no
matter how many times the file is copied, moved, downloaded or uploaded,
you can be sure that it is identical to the original file.

In Android hacking, md5sum is frequently used to verify that critical system
files (which will be used to replace existing files) are exactly as they need to
be before being pushed to the system partition. It is also used to verify a file
after it has been written to memory or the file system.

To verify a file, carry out the following steps:

1. In a command prompt window on your local PC, enter the following
   command to open the ADB shell in interactive mode: adb shell.

   Your command prompt changes to #, indicating that you have root
   access to the file system.

2. Enter the following command at the # prompt to check the hash value,
   for example, of the sample.txt file on the SD card:

   ```
   /data/local/busybox md5sum /sdcard/sample.txt
   ```

   For this file, the output from the hash command should be 4deed-
   76681853806d45e141a96f606dc. (For other files, the output will be a
   similar string.)

3. If the output string deviates in any way from the expected string, you
   need to repeat the process of downloading or copying the file and
   pushing it to the SD card.

   *If an MD5SUM hash does not match, it is very important that
   you do not reboot your device. You must copy the file again until
   you get the expected MD5 hash code.*

4

ROOTING AND INSTALLING A CUSTOM RECOVERY

IN THIS CHAPTER:

- Exploits and how to use them
- Hacking utilities
- Recovery mode
- Using the ClockworkMod recovery application
- Backup and disaster recovery

AN EXPLOIT TAKES advantage of a known vulnerability to allow the Android user the ability to increase his or her level of privilege and access root. Most exploits are found during the bootstrap process covered in Chapter 1. They are discovered by experienced Android or Linux developers and programmers who dream in binary and live on energy drinks alone. When they find a crack in the lockdown that original equipment manufacturers (OEMs) and carriers place on devices, they release the knowledge of the vulnerability and, possibly, an exploit that enables less experienced or less skilled hackers and developers to utilize the vulnerability.

HOW TO USE EXPLOITS

Many of these benevolent hackers release their aids on the XDA forums or other Android community sites. This enables the next level of Android hacker to play with the process for freeing devices from OEM and carrier tyranny. An exploit might be packaged and released by a developer.

> *One of my arguments for low-touch or one-click rooting methods is that they are just a continuation of this thought process. Most of the people who disdain the one-click root method would be totally lost if asked to exploit the ASHMEM vulnerability that enables many of the root processes that are available today. Luckily for the scoffers, Scott Walker created the* psneuter *utility that enables us to take advantage of that vulnerability. Just because something is outside your skill set doesn't mean you shouldn't have access to the benefits and freedoms it brings.*

Exploits can be released to the Android community as scripts, utilities, applications or image files depending on the type of vulnerability being exploited. I consider each of these types of release in this section.

EXPLOIT SCRIPTS

A script is a set of commands that can be run with a single command. A script can be composed of commands and parameters or native code.

An Android developer or hacker who finds a vulnerability or loophole in a device configuration can package up the commands and procedures necessary to exploit it in a script. Using scripts from other Android hackers and developers makes the process of hacking into an Android system much easier. Most OEM-locked devices are eventually hacked with some sort of script or application to exploit a known vulnerability.

Scripts are useful far beyond just hacking. You can create scripts and run them from the ADB shell or an Android terminal application.

> *A terminal application allows you access to the Android command shell from the phone itself. Terminal applications can be difficult to use because of soft keyboard idiosyncrasies.*

Creating a Script

The script shown here is a simple example for demonstration purposes. It may work only if you are already rooted and have superuser permissions.

1. Enter the commands in Listing 4-1 into a simple text editor, such as Notepad. (Note that these commands are explained in Chapter 3.)
2. Save the file as `backup.script` on your local computer.
3. From a command prompt, enter the following command to move the script to your device:

   ```
   adb push backup.script /data/local/tmp/backup.script
   ```
4. Enter the following command to make the script executable:

   ```
   adb shell chmod 0775 /data/local/tmp/backup.script
   ```

Listing 4-1   A simple script

```
mkdir /sdcard/mybackups
cp /data/* /sdcard/mybackups
cat /system > /sdcard/mybackups/system.img
echo Data and System partitions are backed up
```

Running a Script

1. Open the ADB shell and navigate to the `/data/local/tmp` folder.
2. Run the script by entering the following command:

   ```
   ./backup.script
   ```

   The commands in the `backup.script` file run sequentially and carry out the following actions:
   a. Creates a backup folder on the SD card.
   b. Copies everything from the `data` folder to the `mybackups` folder.
   c. Concatenates the `system` folder to an image file in the `mybackups` folder.
   d. Tells the user that it has finished running its commands.

EXPLOIT APPLICATIONS

An application is a program created from native code and compiled to run on the Android platform. Creating clean, effective and safe exploits that run as native applications is significantly more difficult than creating scripts. The developer must clearly understand the vulnerability being exploited, and must also be sure that the exploit does not have undesired results. Because users cannot read the code to see what it does, a good deal of faith must be placed in the developer's abilities. The Android community of hackers are a close-knit and friendly group but nobody likes having their toaster explode from running a rogue exploit on their phone.

You can see by looking at Listing 4-2 that exploit applications are significantly more complex than scripts. The code in Listing 4-2 is from the psneuter utility by Scott Walker, which has been used to gain temporary root access to the Droid Pro and many other devices. There are more than a hundred such lines of code in the utility. It is written in native C code and thus it is more of a full, although very small, application than a script. The temporary root access provided by this script is all the toehold needed to run BusyBox commands and write to privileged areas of the Android file system.

Listing 4-2   Part of the psneuter Utility

```
fdStr = workspace;
if(strstr(workspace, ","))
    *(strstr(workspace, ",")) = 0;
else
{
    fprintf(stderr, "Incorrect format of
      ANDROID_PROPERTY_WORKSPACE environment
      variable?\n");
    exit(1);
}
szStr = fdStr + strlen(fdStr) + 1;
fd = atoi(fdStr);
sz = atol(szStr);
if((ppage = mmap(0, sz, PROT_READ, MAP_SHARED,
   fd, 0)) == MAP_FAILED)
```

Custom scripts and code can also apply themes and interface customizations that developers put together for the community of Android users.

USING A SCRIPT OR APPLICATION ON A DEVICE

Any time you see someone refer to a file as a script or say that a file should be executed from the device, you will follow these steps:

1. Push the file to an area of the file system, such as /data/local/, that can run privileged scripts.

2. Change the permissions on the file to make it executable, using the following command:

   ```
   chmod 0775 <file name>
   ```

3. Run the executable from the ADB shell or a terminal window with the following command:

```
./<path>/<file name>
```

These steps will almost always remain the same, though the location that the file should be pushed to and run from may change.

Z4Root, shown in Figure 4-1, is an example of an application that actually roots while being installed on the device it is rooting. It is a clever and useful piece of programming that does all of the hard work in rooting a device. After installing the Z4root application on your Android device, you run it, click the Root button and all the rooting happens automatically.

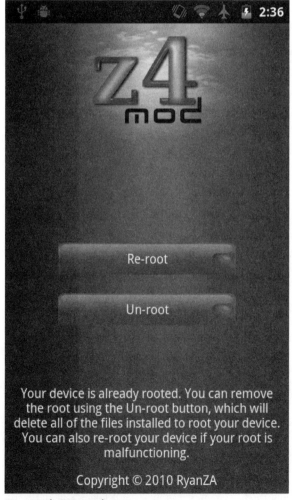

Figure 4-1: The Z4Root application

As with any hacking activity, you take a great deal of responsibility on your own head when you run scripts or applications. Make sure that you either know and trust the developer or that you are willing to accept the consequences of doing damage to your device. You can also lose privacy if the application or script is rogue and harvests passwords from your device.

HACKING UTILITIES

Developers in the Android community frequently compile or create applications that can run on your local computer. They either make hacking your Android device easier or are central to a particular exploit. Sometimes the utility is coded up and created by a skilled developer and sometimes it is "scrounged up" from "leaked" sources at the OEM.

OEM TOOLS

OEM tools are developed by the manufacturer or by a third party for the manufacturer. These tools are used in service centers. For example, RSD Lite is used worldwide at Motorola service centers to install Motorola-signed images on specific Motorola devices.

OEM tools are usually software utilities that can take a complete system image or disk image and write it to the boot loader or file system across the USB cable connection. Examples of such utilities are the NVFlash utility for most devices using NVIDIA's Tegra system on a chip and the RSD Lite utility for some Motorola devices. Using an OEM tool usually requires looking up the instructions on the XDA forums or another Android community site and following them to the letter. Most of the time, the tools have fairly crude interfaces and little or no documentation.

DEVELOPER UTILITIES

Custom utilities from the Android developer community are of mixed quality and ease of use. Some of them are veritable one-click solutions while others perform a single function, such as replacing the user interface or adding other customizations.

IMAGE FILES

An image file is a bit-by-bit copy of a partition (the operating system with kernel, bootloader, recovery, and so on). An image file allows the state, files, permissions and structure to be written to a piece of memory or file system and perfectly replicate the system from which it was taken. One of the uses of image files is to restore a device to the state it was in when it left the factory. In the case of a bricked device, flashing with a known compatible image file is usually the only way back to a fully functional device (see the "Backup and Disaster Recovery" section).

Sometimes the only way to root a locked device is to grab an image of a rooted developer device (one released to an OEM partner for early development) and write it to the locked device's file system. On some devices, the developer does the difficult work in the Android system, changing permissions and installing a different Linux kernel. The developer then wraps this creation in an image file that can be flashed to a non-developer device using an OEM utility or an Android SDK tool, such as Fastboot. In one fell swoop, the device is rooted and prepared for customization.

The Xoom is an example of an (unlocked) device that requires this method. The Xoom was quickly rooted by Koushik Dutta and the boot image file that he released to the community quickly became the basis of much customization and other Xoom root tools and methods. Because the Xoom was unlocked, its bootloader was easily overwritten with the custom image file using the Android SDK Fastboot tool.

> *Much of the really difficult work in hacking and rooting a device is done by developers and released to the community in the form of scripts, utilities, applications and image files. All the average user needs then is the skill set to apply those tools.*

RECOVERY MODE

When your Android device starts its boot-up process, it pulls the bootloader from its storage area and starts the process of loading the Android operating system. By pressing a combination of buttons during the boot process, you can divert the boot into recovery mode. The buttons used to boot into recovery mode vary among devices but the combination of the power button and one of the volume buttons usually forces the device into recovery mode.

WHAT IS RECOVERY MODE?

Recovery mode is an external micro operating system that is used to apply official updates. The default recovery mode looks on the SD card for a file called `update.zip`. When the file is found, it is (usually) checked for a signature to see if it is an update that can be safely applied to the Android operating system. If the signature matches that of the manufacturer, then file system changes contained in `update.zip` are applied and the phone rebooted.

Some default recovery modes also provide the added option of booting into a maintenance mode for clearing the data cache or resetting the device to factory condition.

The recovery system is sometimes contained in its own NAND file system; on other devices, it is just a partitioned location in the overall NAND memory that stores the Android file system. The difference is negligible as writing to the recovery system requires root level access and sometimes it can only be replaced with an external flash process. For most recent devices however, a custom recovery can be installed from the Android operating system once root status is attained.

MAKE IT ALL SO EASY: GET A CUSTOM RECOVERY!

Custom recovery processes go far, far beyond the capability of the default recovery mode. They remove the need for signed or verified updates, so you can install unofficial updates that are released long before OEMs and carriers release updates. Custom recovery processes also provide the ability to completely overwrite the existing Android operating system and firmware. This allows for a custom Android installation and updating or upgrading radio firmware to eliminate OEM bugs or increase capability.

One of the single greatest capabilities provided by a custom recovery process is the ability to do a complete or partial system backup. Backing up the applications, application data and Android file system gives a huge insurance policy to the Android hacker.

> *External complete backups are often called NANDroid backups because NAND memory is used to store the files that contain the Android file system.*

The two most popular custom recovery applications are ClockworkMod and Amon Ra, but they are by no means the only recovery applications available.

There are several ways that a recovery application can be installed. Most devices will accept installation by RomManager or by an update file. You should look up your particular device on the XDA forum to see what others have determined as the best way to install a custom recovery application.

Installation via RomManager

ClockworkMod recovery is installed most easily using the RomManager application by Koushik Dutta. The RomManager application detects the device on which it is installed and decides where and how the recovery can be written. The ease of installing ClockworkMod has made it one of the most widely used recovery applications.

You can also use RomManager to install Amon Ra recovery by selecting the "alternate recoveries" option. You can use any downloaded recovery as an update and use ClockworkMod to select the downloaded zip file as an update.

Installation via update file

Some devices recognize a specially named zip file placed in the root of the SD card. When they are rebooted, they automatically install the update contained in that file. After downloading the desired recovery application, you can rename its zip file and place it on the SD card to be recognized as an update.

USING CLOCKWORKMOD RECOVERY

This section discusses the functions available in the ClockworkMod recovery. Familiarity with these functions will allow you to manage your device with greater peace of mind.

The initial screen of ClockworkMod is shown in Figure 4-2. You can highlight the functions by navigating up and down using the volume up and down keys. On most devices, the power button is used to select a highlighted item (on the Nexus One, you click the control ball). To navigate back from a submenu, the back arrow button or softkey is usual. A few seconds' experimentation usually reveals the navigation buttons.

The following sections discuss each option shown in Figure 4-2. Those with a submenu are discussed in more detail.

> *On certain devices, ClockworkMod has a* +++Go Back+++
> *option at the bottom of each submenu.*

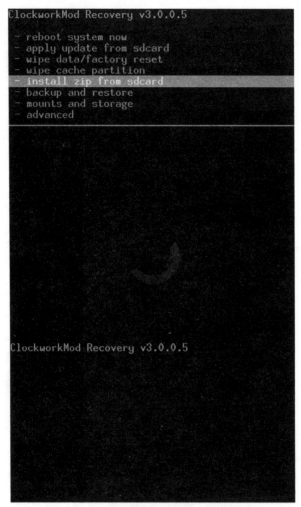

Figure 4-2: Initial screen of the ClockworkMod custom recovery

REBOOTING THE DEVICE

When the "reboot system now" function is selected, the system performs a normal reboot.

UPDATING A DEVICE FROM THE SD CARD

When an official update is released for an Android device, it usually comes as an update.zip file that is automatically applied when the device is rebooted. Some devices can only apply updates in this way.

The "apply update from sdcard" function looks on the SD card for a file called update.zip and applies it. You can apply any update to the file system by renaming the file to update.zip and selecting this option. Instructions for using this method are often specified with updates from the XDA forum.

When you select this function, you are presented with ClockworkMod's safety selection feature (see Figure 4-3). You have to scroll down through a series of "No" options before you get to the "Yes" option. This makes sure that you do not do something dangerous or potentially destructive to your device without being aware of what you are doing. There is little possibility of accidentally selecting a destructive option.

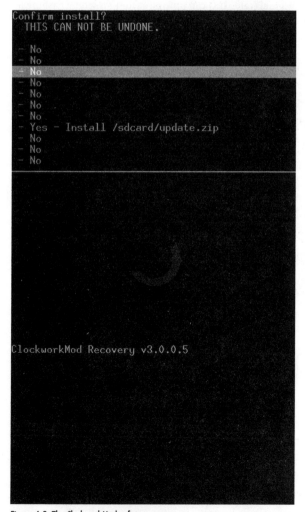

Figure 4-3: The ClockworkMod safety screen

To complete the action, you navigate to the "Yes" option and then press the selector key.

RESETTING A DEVICE TO FACTORY CONDITION

The "wipe data/factory reset" function (Figure 4-2) completely wipes the /data and /cache partitions of the device. This is destructive: it removes all user applications and data and changes the options back to factory settings. All customizations and data are removed from the device. This is the last resort for use in cases where a device is exhibiting consistent failures, force closes or is stuck in some kind of error loop. However, contrary to what the name implies, resetting a device does not restore the /system partition to its original state. This can only be accomplished by flashing an update.zip or executing a NANDroid restore.

WIPING THE CACHE

Wiping the cache is less destructive than wiping the data and can usually be done without any damage to installed applications or user data. However, you should back up your file system before running the "wipe cache partition" function (Figure 4-2). If your phone seems slow and buggy, try this function before resetting the device to factory condition. Sometimes, removing cache data resolves an error state or issues with forcible closing.

This function presents you with the safety selector screen (see Figure 4-3). Select the "Yes" option to wipe the cache.

INSTALLING A ZIP FILE FROM THE SD CARD

The "install zip from sdcard" function (Figure 4-2) is similar to the "apply update from sdcard" function. The update function always looks for a file named update.zip in the root of the SD card. The "install zip from sdcard" function enables you to select any zip file and specify how it is applied.

When you select this function, a submenu appears, as shown in Figure 4-4.

Apply <Zip File>

The file named in the apply option depends on the zip file you select using the navigation function. The default file name is /sdcard/update.zip. If you navigate to a file called myupdate.zip, the first item on this menu becomes apply /sdcard/myupdate.zip.

Figure 4-4: The ClockworkMod install from SD card options

Choose Zip

The "choose zip from sdcard" option allows you to navigate through the file and folder structure on your SD card to locate a zip file. Custom themes and device customizations frequently come as zip files. You use this option to select the file and the "apply" option to apply it.

Toggle Signature Verification

The "toggle signature verification" option allows you to specify that the device should check the selected zip file for a "signature". Most zip files from the OEM or carrier will be signed, as will many ROMs. You should leave signature verification enabled as sometimes this will stop corrupted ROMs from flashing.

Toggle Script Asserts

The "toggle script asserts" option is seldom utilized. It allows or prevents the execution of script commands embedded in a zip file. Most zip files simply update or replace files in the file system. A zip file with embedded scripting can change or alter device settings. Turning off script asserts disables scripting embedded in the zip file.

BACKING UP AND RESTORING A DEVICE

The "backup and restore" function of ClockworkMod (Figure 4-2) is perhaps the most useful and desired item. Backing up data from inside the Android operating system, even on a rooted device, is a complex operation. Clock-workMod can back up all files, applications, settings and data in one operation. The backup file is stored on the SD card where it is mostly safe from any customizations or hacks. This makes for a safety net that is of great value. Periodically backing up using ClockworkMod is a good idea even if you are not an active customizer and hacker. Corruption or data loss from misbehaving applications can be fixed by restoring from a known good backup.

When you select the "backup and restore" option, a submenu appears, as shown at the top of Figure 4-5.

Backup

Selecting the backup option immediately starts backing up your device. While the backup process is running, a progress list is displayed (see Figure 4-6).

The backup file is placed on the SD card in the /sdcard/clockworkmod/ backups folder with the date as the file name. This enables you to distinguish among multiple backup files.

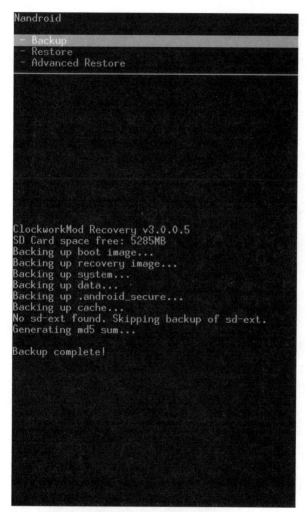

Figure 4-5: The ClockworkMod backup and restore options

It is important that you remove older backup files from time to time. Having too many backup files on your SD card can quickly use up available space. Backup files can be deleted using any file explorer utility, such as ES File Explorer or Root Explorer.

When the backup is complete, you are returned to the "backup and restore" submenu.

ClockworkMod Recovery v3.0.0.5
SD Card space free: 5285MB
Backing up boot image...
Backing up recovery image...
Backing up system...
netperf

Figure 4-6: A ClockworkMod backup in progress

Restore

When you select the restore option, you are presented with a list of all the backup files in the /sdcard/clockworkmod/backups folder. Use the selection keys to navigate to the file from the desired date and select it to start the restore process. ClockworkMod shows a progress bar while the process is running and a completed message when it ends.

Forcing Recovery Boot

Most devices can be put into recovery mode by pressing a combination of hardware keys. Look up the key combination for your device on the XDA forums. If you cannot successfully boot your device, having a good backup and knowing how to put your phone into recovery mode can help reduce panic.

Advanced Restore

The "advanced restore" option allows you to select a particular backup file, again based on the date, and then restore only certain parts of the backup. When you have selected a backup file, you can choose to restore any of the boot partition, the system partition, the data partition, the cache or the sd-ext partition.

Be careful about restoring just one partition unless you know why you are doing it. Partitions usually have related and dependent data. If you restore a data partition that refers to content in the system partition that doesn't exist, it can cause flaky behavior or can lock up your device. In that case, you would need to boot to your recovery partition using the hardware key combination and restore a complete backup.

MOUNTING PARTITIONS AND MANAGING STORAGE

The "mounts and storage" function (Figure 4-2) allows you to manage the mounting of the partitions for various hacking activities, such as copying files to and from the SD card or `data` folder via your USB cable. You will not generally mount or unmount partitions but it allows you to access the SD card while in ClockworkMod and can be very useful.

This function also allows you to format the system partition, the data partition, the cache, the boot partition, the sd-ext partition and the SD card. Formatting involves completely wiping the partition or card and should not be done unless you have a specific reason. If you format any of the partitions and do not restore the contents of that partition, your device will not boot.

ADVANCED FUNCTIONS

When you select the "advanced" menu item from the main ClockworkMod screen (Figure 4-2), a submenu appears, as shown in Figure 4-7. These functions are generally unused except for specialized activities.

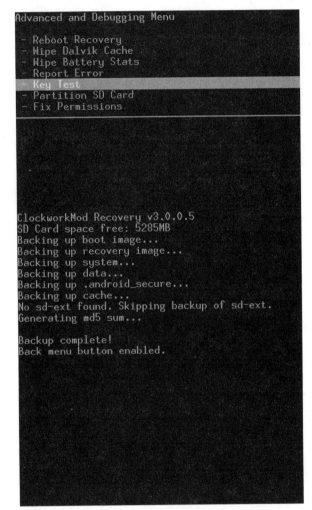

Figure 4-7: The advanced options from the ClockworkMod main menu

Reboot Recovery

This option allows you to reboot the device and return to the recovery process.

Wipe Dalvik Cache

This option allows you to wipe only the virtual machine cache. This can be useful if you have an application that works fine for a while and then suddenly refuses to work at all, closes constantly or exhibits other odd behavior. This is a fairly low-risk option.

Wipe Battery Stats

The "wipe battery stats" option allows you to clear the statistics about battery usage and charge. There is some belief that this can help Android accurately judge recharge and usage control mechanisms. This is generally not true—it only removes historical data from your device. Unless a thread in the XDA forum gives a good reason for removing them from your device, the battery statistics should be left alone.

Report Error

If you get an error while using ClockworkMod, you can use this function to write the error to a log file stored at `/sdcard/clockworkmod/recovery.log`. You can then send the log to Koushik Dutta's team for troubleshooting. When ClockworkMod opens and detects that an error has occurred in a previous recovery session, you receive a pop-up notification asking if you want to report the error.

Partition SD Card

This option allows you to divide your SD card into different partitions. This is a destructive activity that erases all of the contents of your SD card. Only use this option as the result of direct instructions from a how-to guide for your device. For example, some devices can experience a performance boost if they have a large swap partition on the SD card.

Fix Permissions

Every Android application runs as its own user ID. In order to make sure that each application cannot modify any other application's data, the appropriate permissions must be set for each application's space in the `/data` partition. The "fix permissions" function reads through `/data/system/packages.xml` and sets the permissions accordingly.

However, this option does not always yield the intended results and may in fact cause the very application force close problems it is intended to fix. Only run the "fix permissions" option as a result of specific instructions to resolve specific issues. Some how-to guides refer to "running a permissions fix"—this is the option that achieves it.

BACKUP AND DISASTER RECOVERY

In the course of hacking an Android device, it is entirely possible that at some point you will have a moment of panic as a device does not reboot correctly or it appears that you have lost all your data.

Most of the user-created data, such as pictures, documents and downloaded files, are stored on the SD card and are relatively safe from hacking activities that write to and from the system partition. However, you should assume that any hacking or exploration activities could result in the loss of all data.

It's a good idea to connect your device to your computer and copy all the data on the SD card to your computer before starting hacking or exploration. Most recent devices default to "mass storage mode" when connected to a computer. In other words, the SD card is mounted as an accessible drive from your computer's file system manager (for example, Windows Explorer). Copying the contents of your SD card to a folder on your computer will make sure that you don't lose those cute pictures of the kids or the applications you have downloaded from the Web.

To restore such a backup, simply connect your device to your PC and copy all the files and folders back to the SD card.

PRECAUTIONS FOR SUCCESS AND DATA RECOVERY

The best activity to ensure success when hacking is to read more and do less:

- Before starting a process, read the entire thread dedicated to it on the XDA forum.
- Read all of the instructions in a rooting or flashing procedure before plugging in your phone and then read them all again.
- If instructions from a developer mention tools or commands with which you are not familiar, read up on those commands and tools by searching the XDA forums and Google.
- Take special note of people who have messed up before you and what their recovery options or successes were.

Once you have achieved root and installed a custom recovery application, make regular backups using a reliable backup application and the custom recovery application.

The Internet is full of Android geeks willing to assist you if they think you have tried to educate yourself first by reading and searching. It is always better to ask "How do I do X with Y tool on a device that is like Z?" rather than to ask "How do I root my phone?" Having a thick skin is helpful on the Internet as well. Not all geeks have the best social skills and it can show in brusque answers to questions. Maintain your cool, ask your questions intelligently and you will undoubtedly receive the help you need.

BACKING UP APPLICATIONS

Applications that you downloaded from Google Play are automatically restored when you select the "My Apps" button and individually restore the applications. This function is somewhat finicky—most, but not all, purchased apps auto restore, as do certain free ones.

In essence, Google Play keeps track of your purchases and restores automatically at least those applications. On some devices, all of my applications, including free applications downloaded from Google Play, have been restored automatically after a factory reset

If you connect your device to a computer and back up the SD card, it does not necessarily copy the application data. Most productivity applications, such as text editors, office applications and art or media applications, store created files on the SD card in a documents folder or in a folder of their own. Copying everything on the SD card including folders will back up the data from these applications.

You lose all of your application data when an application is removed and replaced. In other words, your progress through "Angry Birds" is not restored even if the application is automatically restored after a device wipe. Backing up user data is one of the primary reasons that root access is so desirable.

BACKING UP THROUGH A RECOVERY PROCESS

When you first achieve root and are able to install a custom recovery application (whether ClockworkMod or another recovery application), you should immediately boot into that recovery process and do a complete backup of your device.

A backup created by a recovery process is a point-in-time backup—it captures the state and data of your device at a particular time. All the applications, application data, user data and system files are backed up. This is the best option for backing up to protect against disaster with hacking.

However, there may be items you want to back up or restore without completely reverting your entire device to a particular point in time. Application-level backups and restores are one of the benefits of being rooted.

BACKING UP THROUGH AN APPLICATION

Applications such as Titanium Backup allow you to specify an application to be backed up. The application can be backed up along with any related data. This allows for specific applications to be restored in the case of them being accidentally removed or having an issue.

When a particular application stops working, you may not want to revert all of your applications to the latest system-level backup. Titanium Backup, and other such applications, allow for individual management of applications. They also allow for nifty manipulation, such as moving applications to the SD card, removing applications completely and cleanly, and scheduling backups. Having a scheduled process that regularly backs up applications, application data and system data will save you a headache when you eventually brick your device.

WHAT HAPPENS IF IT GOES REALLY WRONG?

In the process of attempting to obtain root, it is possible that at some point you will make a mistake and your phone will not boot correctly. There are two generic categories of "broken" when it comes to Android devices:

- **Softbrick** means that the device will not boot completely into the Android operating system but will boot to recovery or bootloader and Fastboot. Any condition that keeps the device from booting correctly but leaves it with the possibility of being flashed and recovered with correct image files is a "softbrick" condition. The most common symptom of a softbricked device is known as a *bootloop* (a condition in which the device partially boots over and over).
- **Hardbrick**, on the other hand, refers to an incapacitated device that is unrecoverable through normal means. Generally, hardbricked devices require specialized hardware methods available only to the OEM to fix, and are characterized by the device not booting at all or bootlooping in a way that prevents commands being sent via ADB or Fastboot.

How your device behaves in each case is very dependent on the device. The procedure to follow in those blind-panic-stricken moments following something going wrong is as follows:

1. Don't panic. Seriously, don't panic. Panic can induce you to attempt the same flawed procedure that bricked your device in the first place. Generally stop and walk away from the device for a minute or two then proceed to the next step.

2. Remove the battery, if possible. Pull the battery out carefully, replace it and see if the device gets any further in the boot process.

On some tablet devices, pulling the battery out is not possible. There is generally a physical key combination (for example, the power button and the volume up and down buttons) that simulates pulling the battery. Press and hold the buttons for a few seconds to see if the device resets and starts booting correctly.

3. Attempt to force the device into recovery or bootloader mode. Look up the key combination for resets and recovery mode.

4. Use the XDA forums and Google to educate yourself on unbricking procedures for your device. If you can find no reference to unbricking your device, post a non-panic-stricken message in the XDA device forum that lets developers know what you were doing when the disaster occurred.

The recovery options available differ depending on what the bricked device will do and to which commands it will respond. If the device can boot into recovery mode, an `update.zip` file or a complete image file can be used to rewrite all the system partitions. In this case, a backup of the device could also be restored. This is why the first step after installing a custom recovery process should be to do a full backup from the recovery.

If the device can boot into bootloader, it may be possible to use Fastboot commands to reflash the system and boot partitions. Search on the XDA forum for posts that contain the required files and instructions. Generally speaking, if a device can be made to boot into Fastboot, it can be recovered.

Some devices can be recovered using OEM or developer tools (for example, RSD Lite for older Motorola phones and ODIN for Samsung devices) to flash image files to the correct partitions. Instructions for using these tools and the files for flashing will be found in the appropriate XDA forum for the device.

5

THEMING: DIGITAL COSMETIC SURGERY

IN THIS CHAPTER:

- How to change the look and feel of Android
- An introduction to tools that you can use to modify your device
- How to modify the airplane mode indicators on your device
- How to create a flashable zip file to share your changes

A MAJOR ADVANTAGE of owning an Android device is that the look and feel, indeed every aspect of the user interface, can be customized to its owner's personal taste.

In this chapter, you learn the basics of theming — changing the look and feel of — Android. Many aspects of the Android interface can be changed, from the colors of navigation elements to replacement icons for applications. Almost any visual element of the Android interface can be altered or replaced completely.

Theming is a complex process that involves getting into the detailed structure of the Android operating system file system. Having achieved root access using the tools described in this book and on the XDA forum, you are now able to begin customizing your device through theming.

This chapter focuses on making changes targeted for your device, such as making the airplane mode indicator more noticeable. The process of turning your changes into a package that can be shared with your friends is slightly more complex. After you make the desired theme change, you learn how to create a recovery-flashable package that can be shared with other Android users.

The process outlined in this chapter is specific to CyanogenMod on the Nexus One, however the process is similar for other devices and other ROMs.

CHANGING THE LOOK AND FEEL OF ANDROID

Theming Android involves editing the graphics (PNG files) and XML files that make up the user interface. Editing the XML is even more advanced than editing the graphics. The Android XML is compiled into binary XML, so you have to decompile it to human-readable text and then recompile it back to binary format.

At a high level, the steps for theming Android are as follows:

1. Extract the files to be edited from the ROM of your choice. Most basic, system-wide themes deal with modifying the images within the `framework-res.apk` file but other changes require more specialized fixes.
2. Decompile the files.
3. Use appropriate editing software to edit the graphics and XML.
4. Recompile the XML.
5. Replace the files into the ROM.
6. Flash the edited ROM using a custom recovery.

These steps can vary depending on what you are changing and whether you are creating a completely altered theme or a theme with minor tweaks. Creating a complete theme will involve iterations of this process many hundreds or thousands of times.

THEMING THE LAUNCHER

The main interface with which a user interacts, the icons, the application drawer and all the other elements are known as the "launcher." The launcher handles not only the look and feel of your home screens and applications menu, but also which applications are visible. While you can theme the native Android launcher, it is often easier to modify an add-on launcher because it shares no resources with the core operating system.

THEMING WITH AN ADD-ON LAUNCHER

One of the most popular launcher replacements for Android is ADW. launcher. It offers built-in theming functionality by allowing users to install easily distributable theme APK or icon packs. ADW users can thus easily switch between themes.

The process of theming a launcher usually involves many of the steps in this walkthrough along with other activities such as creating icons for launched activities (applications) and special file system structures. If you want to create themes for a specific launcher, you need to look up that particular launcher's theming rules and requirements on the XDA forum and the launcher's website. For ADW, you can check out http://jbthemes. com/anderweb/category/adwlauncher/.

TOOLS USED IN THEMING

Theming requires a broad toolset and the skills to match. This list of tools is not exhaustive but gives you practically everything you need to start real hacking at the look and feel of the Android user interface. You will not use all of the tools in this chapter's walkthrough, but you should have them all installed if you intend to continue hacking your device.

APKMANAGER

APKManager is a script that runs as a console application (in a command window). It allows you to carry out easily many of the tasks that would require multiple complex steps if you were to accomplish the same tasks using the Android SDK and Eclipse tools. If you are creating a complex theme from scratch, you are likely to need to use those complex SDK and Eclipse tools standalone. However, for most theming of existing ROMs, and Android in general, the APKManager automates a complex and frustrating process.

What Is an APK?

An APK is an Android Application Package. An APK consists of a folder and file structure along with XML files that define the structure and contents of a package to Android. An APK can be signed or unsigned. Android uses the signature to check for authenticity. Packages also use their signatures to "address" each other. Because of this, it is very important that you follow the instructions about signing and re-signing in APKManager and tutorials on the XDA forum.

Before attempting the walkthrough in this chapter, you need to install APKManager. Follow these steps:

1. Download APKManager from the link at http://forum.xda-developers.com/showthread.php?t=695701.

2. Extract APKManager into a folder.

   It is best to extract APKManager and all the folders into a root folder such as C:\Theming\APKManager. It is important that you have a clean and clear structure for your theming folder because APKManager uses the folders in the structure to decompile and recompile Android APKs.

ANDROID SDK

Refer to Appendix A for information on installing Android SDK and making sure your PC has environment variables for ADB tools. Make sure you install the SDK and set up the environment variables before attempting the walkthrough in this chapter.

ECLIPSE

Eclipse is not required for the walkthrough but is included here for completeness.

Eclipse can be used to edit XML files and the notoriously difficult and semi-resolution-independent NinePatch files (.9.png) manually. Most of what you will do in this chapter is done with APKManager. However, you will want Eclipse for the NinePatch files and complex projects.

You can install the latest version of Eclipse from www.eclipse.org/downloads/. Unless you have a specific reason to do otherwise, you will normally install the classic version of Eclipse.

A ROM OF YOUR CHOICE

For the walkthrough, I will be using the popular CyanogenMod ROM (which is discussed in Chapter 6). The ROM is available at www.cyanogenmod.com or on the XDA forums. These walkthrough steps apply to almost any custom ROM, however. You pull the files you want to edit out of the ROM and make the changes. The files can then be re-signed and inserted into the ROM or pushed directly to your device.

It is a good idea to download your favorite ROM, unzip it, dig into its folder structure and pull out the files you need to edit. This will help you begin to learn the structure and purpose of all those hundreds of files and folders. It will also help you understand steps in the process, such as creating a folder structure on your local computer and then zipping that folder structure for installation.

7-ZIP

APKs, ROMs and many other files are compressed using zip compression. 7-Zip is a tool with which you can open these files and manipulate their internal structure without extracting the contents. 7-Zip has a built in file manager that allows you to navigate through a compressed file, such as an APK, without disturbing the signature on the file.

For this walkthrough, you need to install 7-Zip (from www.7-Zip.org/download.html).

PAINT.NET

Paint.NET is a free and easy-to-use image-editing package that allows you to edit the PNG files that make up the visual elements of the Android interface. Paint.NET is not the only option. Any good graphics-editing package (such as Photoshop or GIMP) will work. Paint.NET is free and is the tool used in the walkthrough. You can download Paint.NET from www.getpaint.net/download.html.

UPDATE.ZIP CREATOR

An update.zip creator makes it easy to create a flashable update.zip file from the files that you create with APKManager. There are many different update.zip creators on XDA, but perhaps the easiest for Windows users is TLC UpdatezipCreator, which can be obtained from http://forum.xda-developers.com/showthread.php?t=1248486.

You will use this program as part of the final step in this walkthrough.

AMEND2EDIFY

Amend2Edify is a program that can alter update scripts created by the `update.zip` Script Creator to be compatible with newer versions of ClockworkMod. The original specification for the update scripts was known as "amend" scripts. With Gingerbread, Google changed the specification to the "edify" script. Edify is more powerful but requires some more complex settings such as knowing where and how to mount the file system in the update script.

Download Amend2Edify from `http://forum.xda-developers.com/showthread.php?t=903598`. Extract the tool to its own folder in your theming folder.

You do not need this tool for the walkthrough, but you need it to convert scripts from the older amend standard to the newer edify style.

THE EDITING PROCESS

This section shows you how to alter the airplane mode icon and status indicator for CyanogenMod 7.0.1 on the Nexus One to make the airplane mode indicators more noticeable. (I find that whenever my phone is in airplane mode I frequently overlook the fact and spend a few seconds puzzled as to why my device will not connect.)

This example changes a single element of the user interface. A complete retheme would involve hundreds if not thousands of such edits. If you download or use themes created by other themers, consider donating to them on the XDA forum. The time involved in creating the tools to make themes and in creating themes is prodigious.

There are two walkthroughs in this section. The first walkthrough demonstrates a method for creating theme files. In the second walkthrough, you see the steps that would be used to create files that could be reused or packaged in a flashable update after many hundreds of edits.

WALKTHROUGH FOR CREATING THEME FILES

For this walkthrough, you target a few specific files that contain the graphics that you want to edit in these APK packages:

- `\system\framework\framework-res.apk`
- `\system\app\SystemUI.apk` (because this is a Gingerbread ROM).

The files outlined here are for a specific device and a specific ROM. Remember that other versions of Android, other ROMs and other manufacturers' devices may require you to amend other APKs.

For instance, if this were an HTC device with the Sense user interface, you would need to edit the `\system\framework\com.htc.resources.apk` file instead of the `SystemUI.apk` file. If you were creating a Samsung Froyo theme, you would edit `\system\twframework-res.apk`. Do your research on the XDA forum.

The best way to find out which APKs contain your desired images is to download a full copy of the theme or ROM that you want to edit and open it or fully extract it with 7-Zip. Once you have the file system available, you can open images in the embedded folders.

Preparing to Edit Files

Before editing system files to create our theme, we must first extract the APK file we wish to modify.

1. Connect your phone to your PC using its USB cable. Verify that the phone is in Debug mode (open Android settings → Applications → Development → Debug).
2. Verify that you have the APKManager folder in your theming folder and that you have installed an image editor, such as Paint.NET.
3. Place your downloaded ROM (in this case, CyanogenMod 7.0.1) in a dedicated folder in your theming folder.
4. Double-click the ROM's zip file and open it in 7-Zip. This will let you browse the file structure of the ROM.
5. Double-click the system folder in the 7-Zip window.
6. Drag the `\system\app\SystemUI.apk` file out of the ROM's zip file and drop it in the `APKManager\place-apk-here-for-modding` folder (see Figure 5-1).

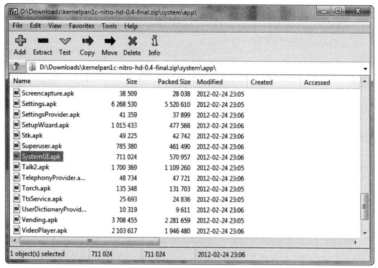

Figure 5-1: Navigating the ROM in 7-Zip, in search of SystemUI.apk

> *The full path for the APK file in the operating system is* `\system\app\SystemUI.apk`. *It is important to note this for later use in APKManager when you want to push the file back to a connected device.*

Loading an Unzipped APK into APKManager

The next step in our theming journey is to load the extracted file into APKManager:

1. Start APKManager by double-clicking `script.bat` in the main APKManager folder.

   The APKManager interface has you choose options using numbers and pressing Enter.

2. Select Option 22 (type `22` and press Enter).

   APKManager reads the files in the `place-apk-here-for-modding` folder and asks you which one is your current project. APKManager works with only a single APK file at a time.

3. Select the number in front of `SystemUI.apk` and press Enter. All of your menu selections from this point will affect this APK file.

4. Select Option 1 and press Enter. You will see a fast scroll of text and then the APKManager main menu will load.

Now you have a new folder, named after the APK that you unzipped or decompiled, under the `projects` folder in the APKManager folder. In this case, the folder is named `SystemUI.APK`. It contains all of the files from the APK. You can navigate through the APK file structure and edit files as you see fit.

Editing the Image Files

You are going to search for and hunt down the graphics that represent the airplane mode icons in the user interface. It can help to change your Windows folder view to display image thumbnails. This will allow you to scroll through the images in the folders and locate the ones you want to edit.

Most of the graphic object elements are located in the `\res\drawable-hdpi\` folder. Resources are found in the `res` folder and the `drawable-hdpi` folder stores the high-density images.

Now that you have all of the "guts" of the APK laid out, you can start poking around for the airplane mode images. The images you want are:

- `stat_airplane_off.png`
- `stat_airplane_on.png`
- `stat_sys_signal_flightmode.png`

Open each of these images in Paint.NET (or another graphics editor). Make the required changes. I removed the image of an airplane and replaced it with the text "AIR." You can do this in Paint.NET by selecting the Erase tool, dragging it over the airplane, and then using the Text tool to type "AIR." Select a font and size that fits nicely in the square.

> *In most graphics-editing programs, press the Ctrl key and scroll the mouse wheel to zoom in and out. This will make it easy to edit the small graphics files.*

Installing a Theme on Your Device

When you have completed the editing process, you can zip up the files and install them on your phone. However, before proceeding with this step, make sure you have created a complete NANDroid backup through your recovery partition, as described in Chapter 4.

1. In APKManager, select Option 4 (Sign APK) and press Enter.

   A new unsigned APK shows up in the `place-apk-here-for-modding` folder.

2. You will be prompted to select whether your project file is a system file or not. In this case, it is definitely a system file so select Y to bypass the signing process for now.

   You can copy the new `SystemUI.apk` file to a master theme folder to create a flashable theme or install it straight onto your device. In this walkthrough, you push the file to your Android device.

3. In APKManager, select Option 8 (ADB Push) and press Enter.

4. APKManager prompts you for a location in which to place the file. You will need to enter a full path and file name. Enter `\system\app\SystemUI.apk` and press Enter. This is the path from which you pulled the APK when you were exploring the downloaded ROM. You want to place your edited APK file in exactly the same place in the file structure from which you pulled it.

5. APKManager pushes the files to their appropriate places. If the device has interface glitches or oddities, don't worry too much about it. You often need to reboot the device before edits show up. If after a reboot, things don't go quite as planned (e.g. you enter a bootloop condition), restore the NANDroid backup that you created before starting this section.

Loading an APK from Your Device into APKManager

It is not always possible to obtain a full ROM for your device. If your phone is rooted, you can pull APK files individually from a device. You then follow the same basic steps of unzipping, editing, zipping, and pushing the file back to the device.

Your next target for edits is the `framework-res.apk` file, which lives in the `\system\framework\` path of your device's file system. You can verify that is where the file lives by opening your downloaded ROM and navigating to that path. Remember that a ROM is an exact copy of the file system on your device; it is good for learning about file system structure and placement.

1. Make sure your device is connected to your PC and in debug mode.

2. Run APKManager.

3. Type 0 and press Enter to select the Pull APK option.

4. Enter the path `\system\framework\framework-res.apk` and press Enter.

   APKManager pulls the `framework-res.apk` file and places it in the `place-apk-here-for-modding` folder in the APKManager folder. This is the same folder in which you placed the `SystemUI.apk file` earlier.

5. Extract the files from the APK using Option 1.

Now you have a new folder, named `framework-res.apk`, under the `projects` folder in the APKManager folder.

6. Open the `framework-res.apk` folder.

7. Navigate to the framework files and edit the appropriate file (for example, remove the airplane symbol and replace it with "AIR").

8. When all of your edits are done, you can zip the APK file by selecting Option 4.

9. Select to indicate that it is a system file.

10. At this point, you can push the APK file back to the device from which you pulled it or place it in your theme folder structure if you are creating a flashable theme.

WALKTHROUGH FOR CREATING A FLASHABLE ZIP FILE

Once you've themed an APK file, you can use the APKManager to push it back to the device. However, if you wish to distribute your theme to a wider audience, you're best served by creating a flashable `update.zip`.

1. Install and run TLC UpdatezipCreator.

2. Navigate to the "Files" tab and click Add to select the files you want to flash.

In this example, we select the files we created in the previous walkthrough.

3. When prompted, select `system/framework` as the target directory for `framework-res.apk` and `system/app` for `SystemUI.apk`.

4. Navigate to the "Options" tab and change the "Script version" field to Edify. This is needed because Google stopped supporting amend scripts in Android 1.5 and ClockworkMod recovery dropped support for amend scripts in version 3.0 (see Figure 5-2).

5. Navigate to the "Script" tab and set the proper mounting point for your device. This is specific to the device, so be sure to search on your device's forum within XDA. Setting this field improperly can have catastrophic results.

6. Now you are ready to finalize your `update.zip` by clicking the "Make an update.zip" button.

Figure 5-2: Selecting Edify script for ClockworkMod recoveries greater than version 3

Once you have created your `update.zip`, you are ready to test it out for yourself. However, to be safe, you should create a full NANDroid backup before flashing. Once the backup is complete, go ahead and flash your update.

Assuming all went well, you have now created your first theme and are ready to share it with the community.

6

YOU'VE BECOME SUPERUSER: NOW WHAT?

SO YOU'VE FOLLOWED the instructions in this book and have obtained root access to your device. Congratulations! It feels good to be free, doesn't it? But freeing your device doesn't inherently give it any super powers until you start tinkering with root-level applications and other modifications.

For most, the first step after obtaining root access is to install a custom ROM. While most custom ROMs are specific to particular devices, several are widespread, cross-platform releases. Here, we present a couple of the most commonly used multi-device ROMs currently available.

After installing a custom ROM, many venture to install a new kernel. Alternative kernels offer many potential advantages ranging from overclocking ability, better battery life and performance, to more esoteric tweaks, such as USB host functionality and sound quality enhancements.

Finally, once the kernel has been updated, many people then install root-level applications that make use of the newly obtained superuser privileges.

The fun in device hacking does not end with simply obtaining root access. Once you achieve root, you have only begun your journey in optimizing your device to fit your needs. With the proper set of customized ROMs, aftermarket kernel tweaks, and root-level applications, you can create a device that is truly your own and capable of far more than the original manufacturer ever intended.

POPULAR MULTI-DEVICE CUSTOM ROMS

As you'll quickly notice when browsing the various XDA device forums, the majority of ROMs that are shared with the community are released for individual devices. However, there are a few notable exceptions. The ROMs presented in this section are large-scale, multi-device releases that often function as the base for further derivative development work.

CYANOGENMOD

If you've heard of Android and you've heard of rooting, you've undoubtedly heard of CyanogenMod. Beginning with increasingly complex tweaks for the HTC Dream: G1, CyanogenMod has grown to become an all-out mega ROM with close to 90 officially supported devices. The ROM itself offers dozens of useful features including lockscreen gestures, a powerful built-in theme engine, audio equalization, VPN support, and much more. CyanogenMod is built from source code made available as part of the Android Open Source Project (AOSP), so extensive modifications can be made to it.

In addition to the official ports, there are hundreds (if not thousands) of unofficial ports and modifications (also known as "kangs"). These unofficial versions typically add anything from support for additional devices to experimental features not yet merged into the official CyanogenMod tree.

The current version of the ROM is CyanogenMod 9. It is built upon Android 4.0 (Ice Cream Sandwich). You can download it from http://get.cm.

ANDROID OPEN KANG PROJECT

Similarly to CyanogenMod, the Android Open Kang Project is built from AOSP-derived source code and incorporates dozens of tweaks on top of Google's own code. At the time of writing, the ROM brings Android 4.0 (Ice Cream Sandwich) to 17 devices, many of which have yet to see the official manufacturer-released update to the operating system revision.

VILLAINROM

VillainROM takes a different approach to multi-device ROM customization. Although some VillainROM releases are compiled directly from source code, most in the VillainROM series of ROMs are actually highly customized versions of the original manufacturer's shipping ROM. Thus, the ROM family varies significantly from device to device.

While the lack of cohesion between supported devices may deter some potential users, this approach also allows for ROM releases to be made quickly after a manufacturer releases a new build of the operating system. Essentially, VillainROM is for users who think that the manufacturer generally did a good job with the shipped software and only wish to have it perfected.

KERNEL TWEAKS

Tweaks to the kernel can give a variety of enhancements to an Android device.

BACKLIGHT NOTIFICATIONS

One of the most popular features of the Nexus One was its multi-colored trackball, which lit up when notifications were present.

When the Samsung Galaxy S line was launched in the summer of 2010, it provided a major upgrade in screen quality and GPU speed compared with the Nexus One. One thing that Samsung left out of most Galaxy S phones was a notification LED.

Thinking outside the box, XDA forum member Neldar was able to simulate LED notification functionality by writing a kernel modification that displayed notifications using the Android softkeys backlight. Neldar's BackLightNotification modification, which has since been ported to other devices, such as the Samsung-built Nexus S, gives users the missing functionality in a very elegant manner. Rather than require a hardware modification or even activating the device's display, the Android softkeys simply light up to indicate that a notification has arrived.

BackLightNotification can be found on the XDA forums: `http://forum.xda-developers.com/showthread.php?t=813389`.

VOODOO ENHANCEMENTS

François Simond, otherwise known as supercurio on the XDA forums, has produced a series of kernel tweaks known as the Voodoo enhancements. As well as providing a more efficient file system, supercurio also decided to improve user experience on the Galaxy S through the development of audio and color tools known as Voodoo Sound and Voodoo Color. You can learn more about the enhancements from `http://project-voodoo.org/`.

Voodoo Lagfix

When it was first learned that the RFS file system used by the Galaxy S line of smartphones introduced noticeable lag to an otherwise-excellent experience, the development community quickly looked for a solution.

Supercurio's Voodoo Lagfix swaps out the RFS file system in the `/cache` and `/system` partitions for the much more Linux-friendly EXT4 file system.

Voodoo Sound

Because the Galaxy S (along with several other Android devices) uses the high-end Wolfson Microelectronics WM8994 DAC, the hardware has the potential for true audiophile-grade sound quality. By allowing for direct, low-level control of the hardware, Voodoo sound gives Galaxy S owners better audio quality than previously imagined.

Several other devices, such as the Samsung Galaxy Tab, Samsung-built Nexus S, and the Asus EeePad Transformer, use the Wolfson WM8994 DAC and can benefit from the enhancements. Furthermore, efforts are underway to port the audio enhancements to other DACs.

Voodoo Color

The Galaxy S shipped with an unfavorable color cast. Voodoo Color gives users direct control of the output parameters of their devices to improve the color cast. It also provides a variety of other visual enhancements.

PERFORMANCE AND BATTERY LIFE TWEAKS

Last, but certainly not least, many people flash custom kernels for performance gains and battery savings. Community-supplied kernels are often undervolted and overclocked, to allow users to get smoother performance and a longer lasting battery.

Many aftermarket kernels also include additional or tweaked governors and schedulers, which alter the way the processor devotes its resources. For example, many kernels default to an "interactive" governor instead of the more typical "on demand" or "conservative" options. As its name implies, an interactive governor generally delivers a more responsive level of performance.

Many kernels swap out the standard CFS task scheduler in favor of the BFS task scheduler, which was created by Australian anesthesiologist Con Kolivas. The BFS generally delivers higher—albeit occasionally less consistent—performance.

ROOT APPLICATIONS

Root applications make use of superuser privileges to alter the device at a basic level.

SETCPU

So you've rooted your device and loaded a custom kernel that tweaks performance and enables overclocking. How do you make use of the additional MHz and run your processor to its fullest potential? Easy: download SetCPU, created by Michael Huang, otherwise known as XDA Recognized Developer coolbho3000.

SetCPU makes setting your minimum and maximum speeds a breeze. SetCPU also allows you to:

- select your clock speed governor and tune its parameters to your liking
- create clock speed and governor profiles for different device conditions (temperature, battery life conditions, and whether or not the screen is on).

If you want to manage your clocks, SetCPU is the way to go.

A donation version of SetCPU can be found on Google Play. A free version is available direct from the developer on the XDA forum.

ADFREE ANDROID

Another popular thing to do when rooting is to remove advertisements. Adfree Android accomplishes this task by modifying the device's `hosts` file. The `hosts` file is a system file (located within `/system/etc`) that is used to map a hostname to an IP address. Instead of relying on a DNS query, the system simply goes to the hostname's IP address, as specified in the `hosts` file.

In order to block advertisements, the `hosts` file is often modified to redirect commonly used advertisement servers to 127.0.0.1, otherwise known as `localhost`. Adfree Android does this and is effective at blocking the majority of in-application and website advertisements.

One caveat to be aware of, however, is that many application developers rely on advertisement revenue as their primary means of generating income. By blocking their in-application advertisements, you are depriving them of their rightfully earned money. Since there is no way to modify the `hosts` file for each application, users that block advertisements using the `hosts` file end up hurting the developers of the applications that they use the most. For this reason, we encourage users who block advertisements to donate to their favorite developers.

Adfree Android can be obtained for free from Google Play or from its release thread on XDA.

CHAINFIRE 3D

Have you ever discovered a killer new game on Google Play, only to find that it is incompatible with your hardware? Unlike PC gaming, where generally all games work on capable hardware, gaming on Android is much more fickle. Games often use texture compression or shaders that are only compatible with GPUs from a particular manufacturer.

Instead of admitting defeat, Chainfire 3D—created by none other than XDA Recognized Developer Chainfire himself—loads an intermediary driver that can accomplish many tasks, given the right plugin. Almost immediately after its release, plugins appeared to allow owners of devices with all chipsets to play games meant for NVIDIA Tegra, AMD Adreno, and PowerVR SGX GPUs.

The intermediary driver allows users to create a setting for each application. Not only can you swap out plugins for each of your games, but you can also enable performance tweaks for different applications, such as forcing 16-bit textures and Z-buffer or limiting texture size (see Figure 6-1).

Figure 6-1: Performance tweaks available in Chainfire 3D

Chainfire 3D can be found on Google Play and instructions and support can be found in its XDA release thread.

TITANIUM BACKUP

And finally, one of the most widely cited reasons to root is the program Titanium Backup. Developed by Titanium Track, the application allows users to back up applications, application data, and system settings. Similar to the previously mentioned NANDroid backup, a Titanium Backup can prevent the loss of your saved game data. However, that's where the similarities end.

Rather than simply making a direct image backup of your device's state, Titanium looks at applications individually and backs them up piecemeal. This is especially useful when used in conjunction with custom ROMs. For example, many custom ROMs require a device to be completely wiped before installation. Normally this would mean losing all applications and data. However, with a Titanium Backup, you can restore individual applications and their data onto the new ROM (see Figure 6-2). A NANDroid backup, on the other hand, only allows users to back up and restore an entire device or a partition on the device.

Figure 6-2: Titanium backup displaying all available applications

Titanium Backup even allows for tasks to be batched and automated. You can backup and restore all of your applications with just a few clicks. You can even set your device to automatically back up your applications to your Dropbox account on a set schedule.

Titanium Backup is available for free on Google Play. A premium version is also available, which adds better batch functionality and more.

II

MANUFACTURER GUIDELINES AND DEVICE-SPECIFIC GUIDES

7

HTC EVO 3D: A LOCKED DEVICE

IN THIS CHAPTER:

- Using the temporary root method
- Using the permanent root method

HTC PHONES HAVE become developer- and hacker-friendly. HTC allows developers and enthusiasts to unlock their devices. You can find out more about HTC's unlock method by browsing to http://htcdev.com/bootloader.

The EVO 3D was one of the first generation of smartphones based on a dual-core processor and running Android. The EVO 3D included a "glasses-free" 3D screen and camera. It shipped with Sense 3.0 and Android 2.3 (Gingerbread). It launched in the US on the Sprint network with access to Sprint's 4G WiMAX network. The HTC Sensation had a similar specification, without the 3D capability, and launched on the T-Mobile network (and on similar 3G/UMTS networks worldwide).

The EVO 3D had a locked, signed bootloader and locked EMMC memory. It was considered to be one of the more locked-down devices released by HTC, but it was liberated a few weeks after its release.

The hacker community developed a temporary root method for the EVO 3D before there was a permanent solution that included S-OFF. After using the temporary root method, the EVO 3D file system would unroot itself and return to a factory state. A semi-permanent root method (known as a "perma-temp" method) gives root privileges until the device reboots. The permanent root solution discussed here removes S-ON and establishes permanent root access on the device.

The temporary root method uses Fre3vo and the permanent root method uses Revolutionary. This walkthrough covers both methods. The reason for covering both methods is to demonstrate the way temporary access was gained and to provide a way to do a full back up before using Revolutionary.

OBTAINING TEMPORARY ROOT

Temporary root was brought to the EVO 3D courtesy of TeamWin. The group developed Fre3vo, a temporary-root-acquiring tool that allows users access to a root shell on their devices. TeamWin is also responsible for a custom recovery and other EVO 3D-specific hacks and customizations.

You need the SDK installed, the ADB to be functioning and the phone to be in debug mode (see Appendix A). You need to download the Fre3vo file from the XDA forum (http://forum.xda-developers.com/showthread.php?t=1149998). The Fre3vo file is an exploit that creates temporary root access to the file system.

This method has you push a file to the file system, make it executable and execute it.

1. Download the Fre3vo file and place it in a folder created specifically for the exploit.
2. Open a command prompt window and navigate to your Fre3vo folder.
3. Enter the following command from the command line:

```
adb push fre3vo /data/local/tmp
```

The binary exploit is "fre3vo" with no extension. Linux-based operating systems (including Android) do not require files to have a certain extension to be executable.

4. Make the binary executable with the following command:

```
adb shell chmod 777 /data/local/tmp/fre3vo
```

5. Enter the ADB shell with the following command:

```
adb shell
```

6. Execute the fre3vo exploit with this command:

```
/data/local/tmp/fre3vo
```

The ADB shell is closed and you return to the PC prompt. You must re-enter the ADB shell to verify you have root access:

1. Enter the following command: `adb shell`.

2. Verify that the shell now has the hash (#) prompt, indicating root level access.

The root state obtained when using Fre3vo is temporary and disappears when the device is rebooted.

USING S-OFF AND PERMANENT ROOT REQUIREMENTS

The AlphaRev, TeamWin and UnRevoked hacker teams all worked together to create the Revolutionary tool, which sets `S-OFF` on the EVO 3D and other phones. Revolutionary is a "closed-source" tool, meaning that exactly how it does its magic is undisclosed. The claim from the developers is that this prevents the method from being patched, or blocked, by OEMs and carriers.

As the time of writing, the Revolutionary tool is in developer pre-release (beta) state and requires you to use a serial number. The serial number is retrieved from the Revolutionary website in the course of running the tool.

Before you start, you need to follow these steps:

1. Download Revolutionary from `http://revolutionary.io`. (You can leave the serial key retrieval form open or come back to it later by clicking on a download link again.)

2. Install and configure the SDK (see Appendix A).

3. Install the HTC developer drivers. (You can download them from the wiki at `http://unrevoked.com/rootwiki/doku.php/ public/revolutionary`.)

4. Download the TeamWin flashable custom recovery (TWRP) from `http://forum.xda-developers.com/showthread. php?t=1192077` (download the zip file not the image file).

5. Download the superuser flashable file (`su-2.3.6.3-signed-efgh.zip`) from Section 99 of `http://forum.xda-developers.com/showthread.php?t=1192525`.

Place all the required files in a folder by themselves to avoid confusion.

Here is a brief overview of the steps involved with getting `S-OFF` on the EVO 3D:

1. Verify that the HTC developer drivers are installed and that you have connectivity between the PC and the device.
2. (Optional) Back up all data (for example, using the temporary root method in the previous section).
3. Run the Revolutionary tool.
4. Flash the custom recovery.
5. Flash the superuser binary.
6. Install the SuperUser application.
7. Run a full system backup from the custom recovery.

The procedure outlined below is fairly safe and brick-proof. However, as with all hacking activities, you accept full responsibility and will void your warranty by running the Revolutionary tool.

RUNNING THE REVOLUTIONARY TOOL

Revolutionary runs on your local machine and communicates with your phone via the USB cable. It does its magic via embedded commands encoded in the binary. You need to verify that you have ADB connectivity (see Appendix A for a refresher on using the `adb devices` command to test connectivity). There is a simplistic interface that runs as shown in Figure 7-1.

The utility will detect the device you have connected (it can be used with a number of HTC devices) and choose an appropriate `S-OFF` method.

The Revolutionary utility will then ask for a key based on your serial number. At time of writing, the Revolutionary utility is in beta test stage and requires a serial number generated by the Revolutionary website. The development team has said that when the key is publicly released, it will not require a beta key.

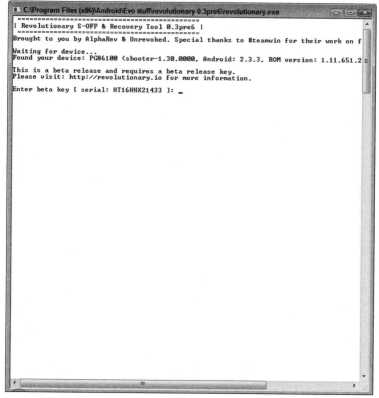

Figure 7-1: The Revolutionary S-OFF utility

To get your beta key:

1. Navigate to http://revolutionary.io.

2. Click the download button for your operating system.

3. Cancel the download window if you have already downloaded the utility.

4. The beta key form is now shown on the page.

5. Enter the serial number of your device as shown in the Revolutionary utility window.

6. Select your device and HBOOT version.

> *Your HBOOT version can be obtained by forcing the phone into bootloader mode with the command* adb reboot boot-loader. *The HBOOT version is listed at the top of the white screened bootloader.*

7. Click the "generate key" button and write down the beta key that is generated.

Now that you have the beta key, enter it into the Revolutionary utility window prompt (see Figure 7-2) and hit the Enter key.

Figure 7-2: Enter the beta key at the prompt

The Revolutionary utility starts its magic. The process takes a little time and your phone will flash and reboot four times. Each time, the Revolutionary utility will prompt you that it is rebooting your phone.

At the end of the process, the utility asks you if you would like to download and install the ClockworkMod recovery. Answer "No" to this prompt as you will be installing the TWRP recovery.

The Revolutionary utility is not always successful at flashing the ClockworkMod recovery. There is the possibility of ending up in a boot loop if you use it to flash ClockworkMod.

After the Revolutionary tool has completed, your EVO 3D will be S-OFF. However, to get full root access, you need to install the superuser binary and a tool to manage SuperUser requests. The easiest way to do this is to flash the SuperUser packages to the file system using a custom recovery.

INSTALLING A CUSTOM RECOVERY

There are two ways that the TWRP (or any recovery) can be written to the recovery partition:

- using Fastboot (see Chapter 3) to flash an image file to the recovery partition
- using the built-in bootloader by renaming the file to the expected update package name (in this case, PG86IMG.zip).

> *The first time I rooted an EVO 3D, I used the Fastboot command to flash the recovery. In haste and with a lack of caution, I flashed the recovery image to the boot partition. This made my phone only able to boot into recovery. In essence, I had a soft-bricked device that took me a full day of sweat and fear to fix. I eventually fixed the issue with a combination of ADB reboot commands and Fastboot.*

The second method is described here as it is safer and less likely to cause issues. You use ADB to push the recovery flashable to the SD card and rename it. This will bypass possible issues with Windows Explorer changing the name and extension of the file.

To flash the TWRP custom recovery, follow these steps:

1. Open a command prompt window and navigate to the folder to which you downloaded the TWRP custom recovery file.
2. Use ADB to push the file to the SD card and change the name with this command:

   ```
   adb push PG86IMG-twrp-shooter-1.0.3.zip /sdcard/PG86IMG.zip
   ```
3. Use ADB to reboot into the HBOOT with the following command:

   ```
   adb reboot bootloader
   ```
4. When the white bootloader screen comes on your device, use the up and down volume buttons to select the bootloader option and press the power button to select. The bootloader scans for the zip file you pushed to the SD card and flashes it.
5. When the zip file has been flashed, use the up and down arrows to select the reboot option and select it with the power button. The device will reboot.

6. Remove any `PG86IMG.zip` file that remains on your SD card. You can do this with a file explorer, such as ES File Explorer, or using the following ADB commands:

```
adb shell
cd \sdcard
rm PG86IMG.zip
```

INSTALLING THE SUPERUSER BINARY

Now you flash the SuperUser recovery binary using TWRP recovery. (If you did not download the superuser binary earlier, download `su-2.3.6.3-signed-efgh.zip` from Section 99 at `http://forum.xda-developers.com/showthread.php?t=1192525`.) You need to push the file to your SD card, reboot into recovery and then flash it from the recovery.

With your device on, connected and in debug mode, enter the following commands to copy the file to your SD card:

```
adb push su-2.3.6.3-signed.efgh.zip /sdcard/su-
   2.3.6.3-signed.zip
adb reboot bootloader
```

> *You can type* `su` *and then tap the tab key to auto fill the rest of the long complex file names.*

1. When the white bootloader appears, use the volume buttons to highlight `bootloader` and press the power button.

2. The bootloader runs a scan for `update.zip` files and then allows you to select the `recovery` option to boot into the TWRP recovery.

3. When the TWRP recovery boots, select the "Flash Zip" option using the power button.

4. Use the volume buttons to navigate to the superuser binary and select it with the power button. The TWRP recovery flashes the zip file's contents and then reboots the device.

When the device reboots, the superuser binaries are in place and you are ready to move on to the next step.

INSTALLING A SUPERUSER APPLICATION

Now that you have a custom recovery and the superuser binary in place, you need a way to handle root and root requests from applications and the Android operating system. ChainsDD, a developer of exceptional talent, has created a superuser management application known as SuperUser. You install ChainsDD's SuperUser application to handle all superuser requests.

1. Search in Google Play for the "SuperUser" application from ChainsDD.

2. Download and install the SuperUser application. (You can purchase SuperUser Elite to thank ChainsDD for his excellent work in the Android hacker community. He works very hard to make this easy for us. For less than a cup of coffee, you can help ChainsDD continue his work for the hacker community.)

3. Run the SuperUser application on your EVO 3D. If the application detects a valid installation of SuperUser binaries, you will be fully rooted with S-OFF.

4. Reboot into TWRP to make a full backup of your file system.

At this point you can download ROMs with customizations and optimizations. Custom ROMs usually have carrier bloat removed and contain customizations to the firmware. Downloading ROMs from the XDA forum can be addictive. Check out one of the aggregate posts (such as `http://forum.xda-developers.com/showthread.php?t=1192661`) that keep track of the most popular ROMs and custom themes.

8

NEXUS ONE: AN UNLOCKABLE DEVICE

IN THIS CHAPTER:

- Information about the Nexus One
- Rooting the Nexus One

THIS WALKTHROUGH APPLIES skills learned in the first part of the book. An unlocked device makes it easy to send files to the root file system and start the customization of your phone. This chapter will make a good read not only for owners of the Nexus One device but also for beginning Android hackers. It is included here as a reference to help you understand the application of the commands and skills from the first part of the book. Read through this walkthrough to understand the process of rooting an unlockable device and the general application of ADB and Fastboot commands from the SDK.

The Nexus One is a Google phone with a vanilla (unaltered) version of Android. It is considered a developers' phone and it can be unlocked using the Fastboot command. The Nexus One was built by HTC and sold by Google. OEMs and carriers usually take a version of Android and modify it to include or exclude features and applications before shipping it on a specific model of device. The Nexus One was designed specifically to highlight an Android installation that had not been altered by an OEM or carrier. The phone continues to be popular among developers and those who value the ease of rooting and developing in an unaltered Android environment.

The XDA forum for the Nexus One can be found at `http://forum.xda-developers.com/forumdisplay.php?f=556`.

ROOT METHODS AVAILABLE

The following root methods are available for the Nexus One:

- the Z4Root one-touch root application, which does not unlock the device
- ASHMEM exploits using `psneuter`
- Fastboot unlocking of bootloader.

This walkthrough uses the Fastboot unlocking method. The Nexus One was intended to be unlocked and used as a developer phone. The Nexus One XDA forum and the Nexus One wiki (`http://forum.xda-developers.com/wiki/index.php?title=Nexus_One`) contain all of the methods and files needed for the walkthrough here.

There are methods for rooting and running custom ROMs on the Nexus One that bypass unlocking the bootloader. The primary reason for using a method that leaves the bootloader locked is to avoid the loss of warranty coverage that comes from unlocking it. However, if you unlock the Nexus One, the process is simpler and you will have a learning experience with a developer-class device.

RESOURCES REQUIRED FOR THIS WALKTHROUGH

Before following the steps in this walkthrough, you should download the following files from the device-specific forum at XDA (`http://forum.xda-developers.com/forumdisplay.php?f=556`):

- Android SDK for the ADB and Fastboot commands
- the Nexus One superboot image file (a boot image with root access that will be written to the boot partition) appropriate to your Android build (to determine the build, open Settings and About This Phone; the build number should resemble "ERE36B")
- the superuser binary
- the SuperUser.apk application
- the BusyBox binaries.

WALKTHROUGH

The skills discussed in Chapter 3 are used here to unlock the bootloader and flash a new bootloader using Fastboot.

> *This walkthrough is for Android 2.3.3. If your Nexus One uses Android 2.3.4, you will need the procedure listed at* http://ndlrazor.blogspot.com/2011/07/how-to-root-android-234-nexus-one.html. *If your device uses any other version of Android, you will need to research the specific variations from the process in this walkthrough.*

The basic steps of rooting the Nexus One and then getting a custom ROM onto it are similar to the other walkthroughs in this book:

1. Unlock the bootloader.
2. Flash a new bootloader with an unlocked file system.
3. Install the BusyBox binaries.
4. Install the superuser binary.
5. Install the Superuser.apk application to control what has root access from the device.

You can unlock the bootloader on the Nexus One with a simple command from Fastboot on your PC. You need to realize though that this method of unlocking the bootloader is unique to unlockable devices. With other devices in this book, you must jump through many hoops just to get the bootloader unlocked. A bootloader from the OEM that is not locked down makes the process of customizing your phone as simple as the walkthrough here.

Unlocking the bootloader on your Nexus One voids the warranty. It is currently not possible to relock the Nexus One bootloader, though progress has been made by developers. You can always go back to a stock version of Android and a stock ROM but unlocking the bootloader is a one-way street. If you want to keep the bootloader locked, you can use the psneuter *method to root your Nexus One (*http://forum.xda-developers.com/ wiki/Nexus_One/Guides_%26_Tutorials#Root*).*

You should note that some unlockable devices can be relocked. The Xoom, for instance, can be relocked as long as the bootloader and the ROM are both signed with the OEM's signature.

PLACING THE NEXUS ONE IN FASTBOOT MODE

The first step is to place the phone in a mode that will accept commands from the Fastboot protocol. This is typically called Fastboot or Fastboot mode. The Nexus One has an intermediate mode called HBOOT, which allows you choose between Fastboot and booting into recovery. To force the Nexus One into HBOOT, start with the phone switched off and follow these steps:

1. Connect the device to your PC with the USB cable.

2. Press and hold the trackball at the bottom of the phone.

3. Without releasing the trackball, press the power button to turn the phone on. Hold the trackball until the white HBOOT screen appears.

4. Verify that the status indicator reads fastboot usb.

   You can also use the volume buttons to select the bootloader option, boot into the bootloader and then select the recovery. For the unlock procedure, you need only the default Fastboot mode.

5. Start a command prompt window on your PC and navigate to the folder where the Fastboot command is installed (usually C:\Program Files (x86)\Android\android-sdk-windows\tools\).

6. Enter the following command:

   ```
   fastboot devices
   ```

   This command works in a similar way to the ADB devices command. It reports any attached Fastboot devices. The output of the command should look like Figure 8-1.

Figure 8-1: The fastboot devices command showing an attached HTC device (the Nexus One) in Fastboot mode

If `fastboot devices` does not return the attached devices, verify connectivity and that the Nexus One shows `fastboot usb` on the HBOOT screen.

7. Enter the following command:

```
fastboot oem unlock
```

This command starts the unlock query on the Nexus One. Select the "Yes, unlock bootloader and void your warranty." option.

The Nexus One will reboot and the boot screen will display an unlocked padlock at the bottom.

FLASHING A BOOT PARTITION

Next you must flash a boot partition that will allow full root access to the file system.

1. Extract the superboot image file to your Fastboot folder. This makes it easier to type the Fastboot command.
2. Reboot the Nexus One into Fastboot mode by powering it on while holding down the trackball.
3. Open a command prompt window on your PC and navigate to your Fastboot folder.
4. Enter the following command:

```
fastboot flash boot <buildnumber>.boot.img
```

This command writes the boot image file that you downloaded to the boot partition.

When the flash is complete, the Nexus One should reboot. If it does not, enter: `fastboot reboot`.

GETTING FULL ROOT ACCESS

The next steps are to install the commands to give the Nexus One full root access and superuser control of the file system. You push several binaries to the file system with ADB then change the permissions on the binaries so they can be executed.

> *Make sure the Nexus One is in Debug mode. Refer to Chapter 3 for instructions on putting your phone into Debug mode. The click path for Debug mode is Settings → Applications → Development → Debug.*

1. Navigate to the folder to which you downloaded the superuser and BusyBox binaries and the SuperUser.apk application.
2. Enter the following command:

   ```
   adb push su /system/bin/
   ```
3. Enter the following command:

   ```
   adb push busybox /system/bin/
   ```

Next, log into the Android shell and change the permissions on these files so they can be executed. If you need a refresher on navigating and using the ADB shell or the chmod command, turn back to Chapter 3 and review the activities there. To make the binaries executable, follow these steps:

1. Open a command prompt window on your PC and verify that you have ADB connectivity with your device. (Refer to Appendix A for instructions on setting up and using ADB.)
2. At the command prompt, enter the following command:

   ```
   adb shell
   ```

   This will drop you into the interactive ADB shell. You can verify it by the # prompt in the command shell.
3. At the hash prompt, enter the following command:

   ```
   chmod 4755 /system/bin/su
   ```
4. Enter the following command:

   ```
   chmod 4755 /system/bin/busybox
   ```
5. Finally use the change owner command to make the superuser binary belong to root. Enter the following command:

   ```
   chown root /system/bin/su
   ```

After the core binaries are installed and the permissions changed, you need to install the SuperUser application (written by ChainsDD), which provides a control mechanism for applications that request superuser access. Navigate to Google Play and download `SuperUser.apk`.

At this point, your Nexus One is unlocked, rooted and ready for more customization.

INSTALLING A CUSTOM RECOVERY

There are a couple of ways to install the custom recovery. The manual way is to download the recovery image file and use Fastboot to flash it to the recovery partition. To manually flash a custom recovery, follow these steps:

1. Connect the Nexus One to your PC and open a command prompt window on your computer.
2. Enter the command `adb reboot-bootloader`.
3. Verify that the Nexus One reboots into Fastboot USB mode.
4. From your PC command prompt, run the following command:

   `fastboot flash recovery <recoveryimagename.img>`

   Wait for the flash to complete.
5. Enter the command `fastboot reboot-bootloader` to reboot the device back into the bootloader.
6. Use the volume up and down buttons to highlight the "bootloader" option and press the power button.
7. The bootloader looks for an `update.zip` file and then allows you to select the "recovery" option with the volume and power buttons. The Nexus One boots into recovery.

There is a far easier way to install a custom recovery, though the manual way is more edifying. Koushik Dutta has created an application, RomManager, that is a companion to the ClockworkMod recovery. RomManager not only provides an excellent way to install the ClockworkMod recovery but is also a way to download and flash custom ROMs.

Download the RomManager application from Google Play. (Purchase the full version as the benefits are many and the developer is both trustworthy and hardworking.)

To use the RomManager application to install the ClockworkMod recovery, follow these steps:

1. Start RomManager and select the "Flash Clockwork" option.
2. Select your device from the list of supported devices that RomManager detects. RomManager will request superuser permissions and the SuperUser application will present you with a pop-up box.
3. Select the "Allow" and "Remember" options. The RomManager will install the ClockworkMod recovery.
4. When the successful flash has occurred, select the "Reboot into recovery" option. Your Nexus One will boot into the ClockworkMod recovery.

At this point, you should use the backup option to back up the entire Nexus One.

HTC THUNDERBOLT: A TIGHTLY LOCKED DEVICE

IN THIS CHAPTER:

- Information about the HTC ThunderBolt
- Rooting the HTC ThunderBolt

THE HTC THUNDERBOLT was introduced to the Verizon LTE (4G) network as a 1 GHz Android device with 768 MB of internal memory. It was one of the first generation of devices to offer 4G speeds on the Verizon network.

The ThunderBolt was also one of the more locked-down HTC devices with multiple levels of security checks and encryption. The locked-down nature of the Thunder-Bolt was intended to keep the device well within the control of the OEM and carriers. However, the ThunderBolt was freed by a combination of the proven psneuter exploit and some new magic in the form of a downgrade firmware that could be rooted.

I have chosen to walk through rooting the ThunderBolt because it is one of the root processes that makes you feel very much as if you are hacking. The reality is that all of the hard work has been done by the developers, such as Scott Walker and Team AndIRC. However, using the exploit and skills you learned in Chapter 3, you will quickly realize you are doing real device hacking.

When released, the device was rumored to be "unbreakable". The hacker community made short work of it anyway. The ThunderBolt went very quickly from being one of the most locked-down Android devices to joining the ranks of completely free Android devices. The walkthrough in this chapter examines each step of the process.

ROOT METHODS AVAILABLE

Most of the root methods for the ThunderBolt follow the walkthrough procedures with slight alterations for updated versions of the phone and changes that come with over-the-air updates from Verizon. It is extremely important that you do your homework on the XDA forum to determine which process is correct for your device version, HBOOT version and Android build.

> *This particular walkthrough is for the MR1/OTA Firmware 1.13.605.7 version. You can check your firmware version by navigating to Settings → About Phone.*

The device-specific forum on XDA can be found at `http://forum.xda-developers.com/forumdisplay.php?f=940`. A good reference thread for this procedure is at `http://forum.xda-developers.com/showthread.php?t=996616`.

Some posts say that the method covered in this chapter is outdated. That is because an easier method is now available. The Revolutionary tool is covered in Chapter 7 and should be used if possible. The method discussed here is still appropriate and still works if the version of Android is the same as originally shipped on the device.

RESOURCES REQUIRED FOR THIS WALKTHROUGH

The following files can be downloaded from embedded links in `http://forum.xda-developers.com/showthread.php?t=996616`:

- the custom ROM upgrade utility, `PG05IMG_downgrade.zip` (MD5SUM: aae974054fc3aed275ba3596480ccd5b)
- the BusyBox binary
- the exploit files, `wpthis` and `psneuter`
- the superuser (SU) binary
- the `misc.img` file (MD5SUM: c88dd947eb3b36eec90503a3525ae0de) for overwriting the eMMC
- the `hbooteng.nb0` image file for replacing the HBOOT (MD5SUM: 6991368ee2deaf182048a3ed9d3c0fcb) (This is the developer version of HBOOT that gives access to more Fastboot commands.)
- the custom ROM upgrade utility `PG05IMG_MR1_upgrade.zip` (MD5SUM: 7960c7977c25b2c8759605be264843ea).

Place all of the files you download into a single folder on your PC. It will be helpful for you to access the files if you create the folder on the root of one of your PC's hard disks, for example, `D:\ThunderboltRoot`. Unzip the exploit files and the BusyBox and SU binaries into your folder.

> *Do not unzip the downgrade and upgrade zip files. They are ROM upgrade utility (RUU) files—signed firmware that will be used to downgrade your firmware and then upgrade after granting* `S-OFF` *to your device. It is extremely important that you do not unzip these files. Place the zip files in your folder.*

WALKTHROUGH

ADB has to be set up before you start this process. Refer to Appendix A for instructions on setting up and using ADB.

> *Read everything. Read the XDA threads. Charge your phone. You can brick your device if you do not follow these instructions correctly. You will void your warranty. You assume all responsibility.*

PUSHING FILES TO THE DEVICE

The first step is to push the exploit file, BusyBox and the exploit image to a part of the file system that is writeable without root access. You will use ADB to push the files and then change the permissions on the files so that they can be executed as binaries.

You will use the ADB shell in its non-interactive mode. When you practiced the chmod skill in Chapter 3, you used the ADB shell in interactive mode. In non-interactive mode, your command prompt does not change to $ after the first ADB shell command. Instead, the command is run on the device and you return to the PC command prompt.

1. Open a command prompt window on your PC and navigate to the folder in which you saved the files.

2. Run the following commands to push the files to the writeable portion of the file system:

```
adb push psneuter /data/local/
adb push busybox /data/local/
adb push misc.img /data/local/
```

3. Enter the following commands to change the permissions on the files:

```
adb shell chmod 777 /data/local/psneuter
adb shell chmod 777 /data/local/busybox
```

GAINING TEMPORARY ROOT

The next step is to gain temporary root access. This is accomplished via an exploit in which ADB checks for the S-OFF and S-ON security flags for the connected device. Scott Walker has wrapped up this exploit into the psneuter utility you have just uploaded to your device.

You now use the ADB shell in its interactive mode (as you did in Chapter 3). In the middle of the process, your ADB shell may seem to freeze—this is expected and you will close your command prompt window as necessary and restart it to continue the process.

Root access using the psneuter exploit is very fragile. It will disappear if your device is rebooted. In fact, it can also be revoked by some device activities. Make sure your device is fully charged and follow only the steps here.

1. Enter the following command to enter the interactive mode of ADB shell: adb shell.

Your PC command prompt should be replaced by the $ prompt that signifies you are operating in the Android operating system with a low or "not root" access level.

2. Enter the following command to run the `psneuter` exploit: `/data/local/psneuter`

   There will be a slight pause and one of two things may occur:

   - You may be kicked out of the ADB shell and see the PC command prompt again.
   - You may freeze at the command prompt and not be able to enter anything.

In either case, simply open a new command prompt window and continue from the next section. It is highly unlikely that you will need to run the `psneuter` exploit a second time. If you do not have temporary root (indicated by the # prompt in the ADB shell), reboot your phone and try the process again from the top.

CHECKING A FILE'S MD5 SIGNATURE

The BusyBox binary (see Chapter 3) contains many commands for the Android operating system, including a command that allows you to hash any file to check its MD5 signature.

When you download a file, you should hash the copy on the file system to verify that it is the correct size and no corruption has occurred. After you write the image file to the part of the file system set aside as storage for particular code, you again hash the data to verify that it was written correctly and with no corruption.

WRITING THE TEMPORARY BOOTLOADER

Now you will use the `misc.img` file you uploaded to overwrite a portion of the ThunderBolt's file system. This will allow you to downgrade the firmware so you can upgrade to a rooted image.

Before you do something as destructive as overwriting a portion of the bootloader, you want to be very, very sure that the data you will be writing matches the known good exploit code. When the exploit was created, it was run through an MD5 hash procedure that generated a one-way hash code that can be used to verify the file whenever it is downloaded or moved.

The process for verifying the MD5 hash of a file is described in detail in Chapter 3. You must enter the following command at the # prompt of the ADB shell:

```
/data/local/busybox md5sum /data/local/misc.img
```

The output from the hash command should be c88dd947eb3b36ee-c90503a3525ae0de. If the output string deviates in any way from the expected string, you need to repeat the process of downloading the file and pushing it to the required location.

> *It is critical to check (and double-check) the MD5 hash here because you are writing to a section of memory with a powerful command. A mis-step or single faulty bit will be the absolute end game for the phone. That is rarely true for rooting procedures.*

Once the hash string is identical to the expected string, you can write `misc.img` to its new home.

1. On the ADB shell command line, enter the following command (see Chapter 3 for more information about the `dd` command):

   ```
   dd if=/data/local/misc.img of=/dev/block/mmcblk0p17
   ```

2. Verify the MD5 hash of what was copied by entering the following command:

   ```
   /data/local/busybox md5sum /dev/block/mmcblk0p17
   ```

   The MD5 hash output should match the following string exactly: c88dd947eb3b36eec90503a3525ae0de. If it does not match exactly, repeat these steps.

DOWNGRADING THE FIRMWARE

In this step, you flash a signed version of the firmware earlier than the one with which your device shipped. As mentioned in Chapter 2, the bootloader looks for a specifically named file for updates to the device firmware. You copy the signed downgrade zip file to the device's SD card using ADB commands.

1. In a command prompt window on your local PC, enter the following command to open the ADB shell in interactive mode: `adb shell`.

2. Enter the following command to rename the file:

   ```
   adb push PG05IMG_downgrade.zip /sdcard/PG05IMG.zip
   ```

3. Enter the following command to verify the MD5 hash of the pushed file:

   ```
   /data/local/busybox md5sum /sdcard/PG05IMG.zip
   ```

   The MD5 hash output should match the following string exactly: aae974054fc3aed275ba3596480ccd5b. If it does not match exactly, repeat Step 2 and check it again. You may also want to download the file again. Do not unplug your phone or reboot it—if your phone is turned off or reboots at this point, it is likely to be permanently bricked. Just keep trying until the hash comes out correctly.

4. When the hash string matches, enter the following command:

```
adb reboot bootloader
```

5. When the white HBOOT bootloader screen shows up, use the volume up and down buttons to select the "bootloader" option and press the power button to select the bootloader. The bootloader locates the signed zip file and flashes it to your device.

6. When you are asked to upgrade, select the "yes" option. Get a cup of coffee and let it do its thing. The flash and reboot can take a long time.

7. When it's done, select the "reboot" option and allow it to reboot.

When the phone has rebooted, use a file explorer (such as ES File Explorer) to locate PG05IMG.zip on your SD card and delete it. This is important as you will later place another signed firmware there for flashing to upgrade the firmware.

GAINING TEMPORARY ROOT TO UNLOCK THE MMC

You are going to follow almost the same procedure as you did earlier when pushing files to the device. Then you will run the two-part exploit to gain temporary root and unlock the MMC.

1. In your PC command prompt window, make sure that you are in the folder to which you extracted all the ThunderBolt exploit files.

2. Run the following commands:

```
adb push psneuter /data/local/
adb push busybox /data/local/
adb push wpthis /data/local/
adb shell chmod 777 /data/local/psneuter
adb shell chmod 777 /data/local/busybox
adb shell chmod 777 /data/local/wpthis
```

3. Run the follow commands to get temporary root:

```
adb shell
/data/local/psneuter
```

Remember this exploit throws you out of ADB shell, so don't panic. Simply reopen the ADB shell and continue with the following step.

4. Run the MMC unlock:

```
/data/local/wpthis
exit
```

REWRITING THE BOOTLOADER

First you push the HBOOT to the file system and verify the MD5 hash. Then you write the file to the MMC and verify the MD5 hash. This is the single most critical moment of this process. If you do not get an exact hash from the MD5SUM command you must rewrite until you get the correct MD5 hash.

If this part of the procedure is done incorrectly, you can completely brick your phone. Go slowly, read ahead and don't panic.

1. In your PC command prompt window, make sure that you are in the folder to which you extracted all the ThunderBolt files.
2. Enter the following command to push the file to your device:

```
adb push hbooteng.nb0 /data/local/
```

3. Open the ADB shell and check the file's hash value using the following commands:

```
adb shell
/data/local/busybox md5sum
  /data/local/hbooteng.nb0
```

4. Look carefully at the output. It must match the following string: 6991368ee2deaf182048a3ed9d3c0fcb.

   If the output of the MD5SUM command does not match the string exactly, you must download the file again.

5. From the ADB shell's # prompt, enter the following command to write the new bootloader:

```
dd if=/data/local/hbooteng.nb0
  of=/dev/block/mmcblk0p18
```

6. When that process completes, you need to verify the MD5 hash of what ended up in the MMC memory block. At the ADB shell prompt, enter the following command:

```
/data/local/busybox md5sum /dev/block/mmcblk0p18
```

   The MD5 hash output should match the following string exactly: 6991368ee2deaf182048a3ed9d3c0fcb. If it does not match exactly, repeat Step 5. Do not unplug your phone or reboot it—if your phone is turned off or reboots at this point, it is likely to be permanently bricked.

7. When the hash string matches, enter the following commands to leave the ADB shell and reboot your device:

```
exit
adb reboot
```

UPGRADING THE FIRMWARE

Now you use ADB to copy the upgrade zip file to your SD card and allow the new bootloader to write it to your device.

1. Make sure you have a PC command prompt window open and are in the folder where you placed the signed zip file.

2. Enter the following command to push the file to your SD card:

```
adb push PG05IMG_MR1_upgrade.zip
  /sdcard/PG05IMG.zip
```

3. Because we only acquired temporary root earlier, we must push the BusyBox binary to the device as well:

```
adb push busybox /data/local/
```

4. Verify that the upgrade RUU firmware matches the MD5SUM hash for the file (7960c7977c25b2c8759605be264843ea):

```
adb shell
/data/local/busybox md5sum /sdcard/PG05IMG.zip
```

If the hash strings do not match, download the upgrade zip file and push it to the SD card again until they do match.

5. Once the file is correctly written to your SD card, you can let the new bootloader write the new firmware:

```
exit
adb reboot bootloader
```

When the white HBOOT screen boots up, use the volume and power buttons to select the "bootloader" option. The bootloader will check for PG05IMG.zip and flash it. Again when asked to upgrade, select "yes" and go for a cup of coffee—it can take a while. When the flashing is completed, reboot the device and remove PG05IMG.zip from your SD card.

At this point you are running a device that is S-OFF—it has the security flag off and is running release (as opposed to developer) firmware.

Download SuperUser.apk from Google Play by searching for the SuperUser application. You can also purchase and install RomManager to have access to custom recoveries and custom ROM firmware for flashing.

If you were to accept a download pushed over the air (OTA) from your carrier, you would be very likely to undo all of your hard work: it will unroot and remove the custom firmware. It is best not to accept OTA updates. However, if you install a custom ROM, you are unlikely to see OTA updates, as most ROMs block them. Most custom ROMs release their own updates based on the OTAs.

10

DROID CHARGE: FLASHING WITH ODIN

IN THIS CHAPTER:
- Information about the Droid Charge
- Rooting the Droid Charge

THE DROID CHARGE is a well-rounded Android smartphone with a high-contrast display and access to Verizon's LTE (4G) network.

Customizing the ROM and firmware on a Droid Charge involves steps rather different from using ADB to send and receive commands and files to the device. Although ADB can be used to communicate with a Samsung (as with nearly all Android devices), most firmware modification procedures on Samsung devices use a software suite known as ODIN. Similar to the Fastboot protocol, ODIN is a tool that takes firmware packages (rooted ROMs, recoveries and other customizations) and writes them to the memory of a Samsung device. ODIN makes for a fairly easy rooting process. While it is more user-friendly than the command line, ODIN itself is not terribly intuitive and requires some basic explanation of the interface.

ODIN flashes to your phone's file system specially formatted packages in
.tar.md5 format. The easiest way to accomplish root-level access is to flash
the ClockworkMod recovery and then use the recovery to install the rooted
ROM of your choice.

*Never flash a package that you do not know is intended for your
device and firmware (bootloader) version.*

RESOURCES REQUIRED FOR THIS WALKTHROUGH

You can download all the required pieces of software from http://
forum.xda-developers.com/showpost.php?p=15897406.
At a minimum, you need:

- drivers for the Droid Charge
- ODIN 3.x
- ClockworkMod in a format for ODIN to flash
- a rooted customized ROM to flash with ClockworkMod.

*There are complete packages for the Droid Charge that include a
rooted ROM and ClockworkMod. Flashing an all-in-one package,
such as the one listed in the XDA forum post at http://forum.
xda-developers.com/showpost.php?p=15897406 will
result in a single flash step instead of multiple steps.*

WALKTHROUGH

If you downloaded a Charge Kit from http://forum.xda-developers.
com/showpost.php?p=15897406, you need to extract ODIN to a folder
of its own somewhere on your machine. This folder is primarily for running
the ODIN utility; try not to put flashable files and other files into it.

CONNECTING THE DEVICE TO ODIN

Run the ODIN utility by double-clicking the ODIN executable. You should
see the utility as in Figure 10-1.

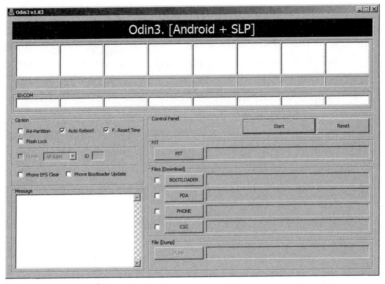

Figure 10-1: The ODIN utility

For the phone to communicate with the ODIN utility, it needs to be in download mode. Put the phone in download mode by following these steps:

1. Pull the battery from your Droid Charge.

2. Plug your Droid Charge into your computer with the USB cable. The phone will take its power from the PC in most cases. (See the "Troubleshooting" section if you have a problem.)

3. Hold the volume down button until you see a large yellow triangle.

4. Your phone is in download mode and ODIN should now show a connected device in the ID:COM window.

FLASHING THE DEVICE

This stage involves browsing to a file you want to flash and using ODIN to flash it to the device.

1. Open the ODIN utility on the PC.

2. Click the check box in front of the PDA button.

3. Click the PDA button. You are presented with a file selection dialog.

> *The button you use is the PDA button. It cannot be stressed enough that you do not use any other button to flash your phone.*

4. Navigate to the file you wish to flash to your Droid Charge. This could be an all-in-one ROM–Root–Recovery package or the ClockworkMod file.

5. Select a .tar.md5 file; its path is placed in the text box to the right of the PDA button.

6. Uncheck the "Auto Reboot" check box (below the ID:COM boxes).

7. Press the "Start" button.

ODIN will show the download process. Do not interrupt the process. When the download has completed, ODIN will display a blue "Restart" and then show a green "Pass" in the ID:COM box.

If "Pass" does not show, you need to start troubleshooting the flash process. Using ODIN is a fairly safe and straightforward activity. If you experience issues, skip to the "Troubleshooting" section.

8. Disconnect your phone to reboot it. If you inserted the battery for troubleshooting, you will need to pull the battery out as well.

- If the package you installed with ODIN was a recovery package, you can now boot into recovery to install a custom rooted ROM. Use the information in Chapter 3 on ClockworkMod to install a custom ROM with it.

- To boot into recovery, press the home, volume up and power buttons all at the same time while booting. When the Samsung logo appears, you can release the power button but continue to press the other buttons.

TROUBLESHOOTING

If your ODIN interface does not flash the green "Pass" in the ID:COM rectangle, consider some of these troubleshooting tips:

- If the device seems to shut down without completing the process, there may be a problem with the amount of power being sent to the device via the USB cable. Try changing USB ports and ensure that you are using a rear USB port.

- Only use a USB port directly in the computer, never a USB hub or a "front" USB port. If you do not use a main USB port, there is a possibility of interference and there may not be sufficient voltage for the flash to complete.

- Verify that the USB cable you are using is a data cable and not just a charging cable. Try a different combination of USB cable and port.

- If there is a problem when the phone is connected to ODIN and in Download mode, reinsert the battery for the flash. After you flash your package, remove the battery to restart the device.

- ODIN does not like to share, so turn off all other software. Disable or turn off anti-virus software, firewalls and other security software.

- There is always the possibility of a bad download of your flash packages. Download your package again, whether it is an all-in-one package or a recovery or ROM package.

11

NEXUS S: AN UNLOCKED DEVICE

IN THIS CHAPTER:

- Information about the Nexus S
- Rooting the Nexus S

THE NEXUS S is Google's second flagship vanilla Android smartphone. Periodically, Google releases one phone in conjunction with a device manufacturer. These phones feature "Nexus" branding. Nexus phones are vanilla Android installations, with no interface or operating system customizations. Unlocked or unlockable bootloaders and freely available driver binaries make the Nexus phones highly prized by the hacking and hobbyist communities.

Unlocked devices are usually locked from the factory but have firmware in place that allows them to be unlocked with Fastboot commands. The Nexus S follows this pattern. Unlike the Google Nexus One, the Nexus S allows the bootloader to be relocked as well. After unlocking the Nexus S, it is fairly straightforward to use native Fastboot flashing functionality to flash the recovery or firmware of your choice.

Nexus phones are unlocked because Google sees them as developer devices. Developers need to be able to access the Android operating system at a very low level. When a developer is creating an application, there needs to be a common device that can be considered to be the reference device for a particular version of Android.

CONNECTING THE DEVICE TO A PC

The Nexus S may require some special attention to connect to your PC so that ADB and Fastboot commands can be used. Be sure to download and install the correct drivers for your Nexus S from the reference thread at http://forum.xda-developers.com/showthread.php?t=935819.

After installing the third-party drivers, you should thoroughly test ADB and Fastboot connectivity. Refer to Appendix A for connectivity tests and Android SDK installation instructions.

RESOURCES REQUIRED FOR THIS WALKTHROUGH

Download the required files to a dedicated folder on your PC to make it easier to perform the flashing:

- drivers for Fastboot and ADB connectivity
- a custom recovery, such as ClockworkMod
- the SuperUser binary and application from the reference thread on the XDA forum.

WALKTHROUGH

UNLOCKING THE DEVICE

Follow these steps to unlock the Nexus S and prepare it for flashing a custom recovery.

1. Back up everything on your device.

   Unlocking the Nexus will completely erase all the data on the device as well as on the SD card. Connect the device to your PC, mount the SD card as storage and copy all its contents to your PC. When you have completed the re-rooting procedure, you will be able to copy back the contents of your SD card.

2. Put your Nexus S in Fastboot mode:

   a. Start with the device off.

   b. Power it on while pressing the volume up and power buttons.

   The device should boot to the white Fastboot screen with the skating Androids.

3. From a command prompt window on your PC, run the following command to unlock your Nexus S:

   ```
   fastboot oem unlock
   ```

4. Your device will prompt you to verify that you want to unlock. Remember that unlocking not only erases your device, it also voids your warranty.

5. Press the volume up button and then the power button to verify the unlock.

The device will wipe and reboot. When the phone reboots, it will be unlocked and can be flashed with the Fastboot command.

FLASHING THE DEVICE WITH A RECOVERY

Next you will use the Fastboot command to flash the device with the ClockworkMod recovery. Make sure that you download the recovery appropriate for the Nexus S. The reference thread on the XDA forum will have a link to the latest version.

1. Put the Nexus S in Fastboot mode.

2. With the device connected to your PC, enter the following command from the folder to which you downloaded ClockworkMod:

   ```
   fastboot flash recovery recovery-clockwork-crespo.img
   ```

   Note: The name of the image file may include a version number that will change with the version of the recovery.

After the successful flash, you can reboot into recovery by powering the Nexus on while holding the volume up and power button. When the white HBOOT screen comes up, select the recovery option.

FLASHING THE DEVICE WITH THE SUPERUSER APPLICATION

1. Use the ClockworkMod mount USB option (see Chapter 4) to mount the SD card as mass storage.

2. Copy `SuperUser.zip` to the root of the SD card.

3. Use the "Install Zip" option to select the SuperUser application and flash it to your Nexus S.

At this point, your Nexus S is unlocked and rooted. However, it will replace the recovery on reboot thanks to the file system protection system: code in the boot process will detect that the recovery has been altered and rewrite the default recovery to the recovery partition. To change this behavior, follow these steps:

1. Download a root permissions file explorer, such as the Root File Explorer, that can mount the file system for reading and writing.

2. Mount the file system as writable (in Root File Explorer, click the gray "Mount r/w" button).

3. Navigate to the `/etc` folder.

4. Rename the `recovery-install.sh` file to `recovery-install.old`.

5. Open Google Play, download RomManager and install it.

6. Use the "Install Clockwork Recovery" option to reinstall Clockwork-Mod recovery.

At this point, ClockworkMod should be permanent and you are rooted and ready to install custom ROMs or other customizations.

12

MOTOROLA XOOM: AN UNLOCKED HONEYCOMB TABLET

IN THIS CHAPTER:

- Information about the Motorola Xoom
- Rooting the Motorola Xoom

THE XOOM IS an unlocked tablet that was released with the Honeycomb (Android 3.0) operating system. It was one of the first tablets released with this version of Android.

The Xoom is considered a developers' device. As with its Google Experience Device stablemates, it is easily unlocked using the Fastboot commands. Rooting and flashing custom ROMs is easy. However, the Honeycomb source code was released late by Google, at the same time as the source for Ice Cream Sandwich (Android 4.0). Both Honeycomb and Ice Cream Sandwich have nearly identical driver requirements, so most developers did not see the point in building custom ROMs for an inferior OS version. This means that there are fewer custom ROMs for it than there are for other versions of Android for which developers have access to the source code repositories.

RESOURCES REQUIRED FOR THIS WALKTHROUGH

To carry out the procedure, you need the following setup:

- The Xoom needs to be in Debug mode.
- ADB must be installed and functioning.
- An external SD card must be installed on the Xoom.
- You must download the following files from the XDA forum at `http://forum.xda-developers.com/showthread.php?p=17135571`:
  - the root zip file
  - the image recovery file.

WALKTHROUGH

The basic steps of rooting the Xoom are as follows:

1. Place the root zip file on the SD card.
2. Unlock the Xoom.
3. Flash the recovery to the Xoom.
4. Use the recovery to flash a universal root.

PUSHING THE ROOT FILE TO THE SD CARD

You need to download the universal root file from the link at `http://forum.xda-developers.com/showthread.php?p=17135571` and place it on the SD card. You may need to use an adapter to connect the SD card as an external storage medium. Once you have copied `xoom-universal-root.zip` to the SD card, you can place the SD card in your Xoom.

UNLOCKING THE XOOM

If you have not done so previously, you need to unlock the Xoom bootloader. The process is fairly simple but requires careful reading of the Xoom screen during the process. Follow these steps to unlock the Xoom bootloader.

> *Unlocking your device will completely erase the data on it (including data on the SD card). The internal memory design and the way the device unlocks completely resets the Xoom to factory condition. You will lose all data.*

1. Connect the Xoom to your PC with the USB cable and verify that the Xoom is in Debug mode.

2. Open a command prompt window on your PC and enter the following command to boot the Xoom into Fastboot mode:

   ```
   adb reboot bootloader
   ```

   If this step does not work make sure that ADB is set up correctly (refer to Appendix A).

   You can also get the Xoom into Fastboot mode by powering it off and pressing the power and volume up buttons until Fastboot mode appears.

In Fastboot mode, the Xoom can accept the Fastboot commands that you will use to flash the custom recovery. This is the mode you would use to recover a softbrick of any kind. If you can get the device to boot to Fastboot mode, you can generally flash some sort of usable ROM or recovery and get yourself out of softbricks and boot loops. The Xoom is fairly bulletproof in this regard.

With the Xoom in Fastboot mode, you can unlock the bootloader by following these steps:

1. In a command prompt window, enter the following command:

   ```
   fastboot oem unlock
   ```

2. Read the Xoom screen carefully. There is a warning that you are voiding your warranty and that you will lose all data. Pay close attention to the steps necessary to verify the unlock. You will use the volume up and down buttons to verify or back out of the process.

After unlocking, the Xoom will reboot and function as usual. There is no difference in the device at this point except that the bootloader is unlocked.

FLASHING THE DEVICE WITH A RECOVERY

The next step is to flash the custom version of the ClockworkMod recovery. This custom version takes into account the Xoom's peculiar use of internal memory as an SD card. In essence, it completely skips the need for an SD card. You should have downloaded a file named `solarnz-<versionnumber>.img`.

You cannot flash a zip file from Fastboot mode—you can only flash image files. You use zip files with ClockworkMod or some other custom recovery.

1. Put the Xoom back into Fastboot mode: `adb reboot bootloader`.
2. Enter the following command:

```
fastboot flash recovery solarnz-######.###.img
```

It is important that the file name you enter is exactly the name of the file you downloaded. It is also extremely important that you use the "recovery" keyword with the Fastboot flash command to ensure that you flash the correct partition.

The Xoom will report that it is flashing the file and then indicate when the process is complete. At this point, your Xoom has the ClockworkMod recovery installed and can be booted into the recovery for customizations, such as flashing custom kernels, themes, or startup animations and full custom ROMs.

Do not reboot your Xoom until you have flashed it with a universal root or you will have to re-flash the ClockworkMod file to the recovery partition. If you do not do this, `/system/recovery-from-boot.p` will revert your recovery partition to the default recovery upon your next reboot.

FLASHING THE DEVICE WITH A UNIVERSAL ROOT

To achieve rooted full access to the existing file system, you need to flash the universal root package that you downloaded. This package contains the files for the rooted file system and the superuser binaries for accessing system-level permissions and files.

This stage has a bit of tricky timing. If you miss the timing, you will need to reflash the ClockworkMod recovery. The recovery system has a built-in auto-restore feature. The overview is that you use the Fastboot command to reboot the Xoom; when you see the Motorola logo, you press volume down and then volume up to bump the system into the new recovery.

Follow these steps to flash the universal root file:

1. If you have not yet done so, copy the universal root zip file to the root of your SD card (not to a folder) and insert the card into the Xoom.

   Your Xoom should show the successful message from flashing the ClockworkMod recovery file.

2. Enter the following command into the command prompt window to reboot the Xoom:

```
adb reboot
```

3. When you see the Motorola logo, count to three and press the volume down button. You should see "Android Recovery" appear on the screen.

4. Press the volume up button to boot into the newly installed Clockwork-Mod recovery.

> *If you miss the opportunity to boot into the recovery, you may have to go back and reflash the ClockworkMod recovery to the recovery partition because* /system/recovery-from-boot.p *will revert to the default recovery.*

5. Use the volume buttons to select the "Install Zip from sdcard" option and press the power button.

6. Select the "Choose Zip" option.

7. Navigate with the volume up and down buttons to the universal root zip file you placed on the SD card and select it with the power button.

8. Confirm the installation.

When the installation has finished, navigate back to the main Clock-workMod menu and reboot the Xoom.

Your Xoom is now unlocked and rooted. You can use the volume up key or the command adb reboot recovery to boot into recovery and boot the ROMs and customizations you want. Check out the XDA Xoom forum for the latest and greatest from the hard-working developers of ROMs, kernels, and customizations.

Refer to Chapter 4 for specific instructions on using ClockworkMod recovery.

13

NOOK COLOR: ROOTING WITH A BOOTABLE SD CARD

IN THIS CHAPTER:

- Information about the Nook Color
- Rooting the Nook Color

THE NOOK COLOR, released by Barnes and Noble, was originally intended to be an eReader based on Android. In the hands of Android hackers, it quickly became one of the best-value tablets that could be purchased. Once rooted and with a custom ROM, it was transformed into a usable and fully functional Android tablet.

Because of the nature of the device startup routine (it does not support the Fastboot protocol), a slightly different method is needed to root and ROM the Nook Color compared to other Android tablets. You use an SD card that has been made bootable by flashing an image file to it. When the SD card is inserted into the Nook Color, it takes precedence over the Nook Color native boot routine and the files on the SD card are booted. This allows you to do fun stuff, such as writing a native custom recovery to the EMMC memory and root the device.

This method can also be used for other minor brand or unbranded varieties of Android tablets (usually they have no Google license or Google Play support). The details change but the core skills are the same. Be sure to read up on your device before starting this or any rooting process.

RESOURCES REQUIRED FOR THIS WALKTHROUGH

To carry out the procedure, you need the following setup:

- a registered Nook Color, version 1.1
- an SD card that you can completely wipe
- a dedicated SD card writer (most built-in SD card writers will not work—get one that plugs into your USB port)
- a Gmail account that you have linked to YouTube
- the Auto-Nooter image file from `http://forum.xda-developers.com/showthread.php?t=942424`
- the Win32DiskImage image writer from `https://launchpad.net/win32-image-writer/+download`.

The Auto-Nooter is a convenient little piece of software that was built by developers at Nookdevs.com. The Auto-Nooter does most of the hard work when the Nook Color boots from it. After you have booted the Nook Color from the Auto-Nooter SD card, the SD card can be reformatted and removed or used as added storage.

WALKTHROUGH

The high-level steps of the process are:

1. Burn (write) the custom bootable image to the SD card using your PC.
2. Boot the Nook Color device using the SD card.
3. Allow the auto-root routine to complete.

This walkthrough is for the Nook Color version 1.1. If you have a different version, read up at the XDA forum to find the differences. The primary differences are in the files used—the steps are virtually the same.

CREATING A BOOTABLE SD CARD

Remember that this process can also be used for other versions of the Nook Color and minor brand or unbranded Android tablets.

1. Run the Win32DiskImage writer program that you downloaded.
2. Click the folder button to navigate to the Auto-Nooter image file.
3. Double-click the image file.
4. Click on the drop-down with drive letters. Select the drive letter that corresponds to your SD card.

   You can double-check the drive letter of your SD card by opening Windows Explorer and looking for the SD card drive letter there.

   Make sure that you select the correct drive letter. You don't want to overwrite a data partition or another external storage device. This process irrevocably deletes all content on the selected drive.

5. Click the "Write" button and let the image be written to the SD card.
6. When the writing process is complete, verify the contents of the SD card by using Windows Explorer to open it. You should see the following items:

```
MLO
u-boot.bin
uImage
uRamdisk
```

BOOTING THE DEVICE FROM THE SD CARD

These steps guide you through booting the Auto-Nooter on the Nook Color and wrapping up the root and boot process.

1. Turn off your Nook Color completely.
2. Place the SD card to which you have just written the Auto-Nooter into the Nook Color.
3. Plug the USB cable from your computer into the Nook Color. This will cause the Nook Color to turn on and boot from the SD card.

   The screen will be off during the Auto-Nooter booting. You will not see anything on the screen. Be patient. If you are using the Nook Color cable, the LED will blink but this is irrelevant to the process.

4. Your computer will indicate that a new device has been plugged in. Cancel any request for drivers from your PC.

When the process is done, you will see a new boot animation. Pull the SD card out of the Nook Color to ensure it does not boot from the SD card again.

MAKING THE DEVICE MORE USABLE

At this point, the hard work has been done—your Nook Color is rooted. However, to make it more usable you need to enable:

- Google account integration, so you have Google Play access
- Softkeys, so you have access to the Android Back, Home, Menu and Search keys.

The process of setting up and enabling Google account integration uses a clever "back door". It uses the sign-in integration between YouTube and Google.

1. On boot, tap the Android.

2. Tap the "Skip Sign in" button.

3. Enable the location services option.

4. Connect to a known good Wi-Fi connection.

5. Launch the YouTube application from the "Extras" menu button.

6. Tap the Menu button to the right of the up arrow.

7. Tap "My Channel" and log in with your Google account.

8. Exit YouTube and launch Gmail from the same "Extras" menu.

9. Synchronize your Gmail account and exit. This could take a few minutes, so be patient.

10. Open up Google Play and accept the terms of service.

11. Download an application to verify that it works.

If the download stalls without installing the application, reboot the Nook and try again.

You need to set the Softkeys so that you have access to the Home, Back, Menu and Search keys native to Android.

You need to set the Softkeys program as your default launcher, to cause it to load automatically. Select the Softkeys application from your applications drawer and select the check box that sets the softkey actions to be remembered as the defaults. Next, set the Home softkey to call your real launcher program by pressing the Menu button and selecting your launcher applications.

SETTING UP ANDROID SDK AND ADB TOOLS

THIS APPENDIX HELPS you to set up the Android developer tools you use to root and hack your phone.

INSTALLING THE JAVA DEVELOPMENT KIT

The first step to getting access to the Android developer tools is to download the Java Development Kit (JDK). Although you do not use the tools provided by the JDK, it must be installed for you to be able to install the Android SDK.

1. Navigate your browser to `www.oracle.com/technetwork/java/javase/downloads/` (see Figure A-1). Any current version will work with Android SDK.

Figure A-1: Downloading the JDK

2. Click the Java Platform (JDK) button.

3. Click to accept the licensing agreements and then select the correct installer for your computer. Most Windows users will click on Windows x86. If you have 64-bit Windows, click the x64 link.

4. Download the installer to a location you can easily find on your computer.

5. Run the installer executable.

6. Click through the JDK installation wizard accepting all the defaults.

INSTALLING THE ANDROID SDK

Now you can download and run the installer for the Android SDK.

1. Navigate your browser to `http://developer.android.com/sdk/`.
2. Download the appropriate package for your operating system (Windows users should download the installer executable).
3. Run the downloaded package.
4. Click through the installer.

   Take special note of where the Android SDK is installed. You can change the path but it is better to accept the default path. For 64-bit systems, the default path should be something like `C:\Program Files(x86)\android\android-sdk-windows\`. For 32-bit systems, the only difference will be the absence of "(x86)" from the path.

When the wizard completes, it will have a check mark to start the SDK manager. You use the SDK manager to download the required platform tools (i.e. ADB and others). You can also launch the SDK manager from the operating system, as shown in Figure A-2.

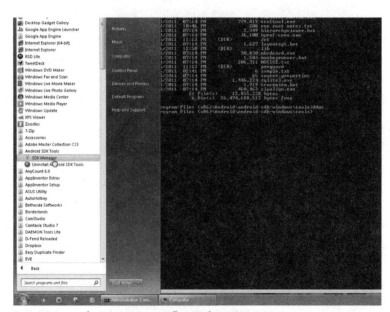

Figure A-2: Starting the SDK manager manually in Windows

INSTALLING THE PLATFORM TOOLS

When the SDK Manager starts, it finds out from Google what packages are available for download and then presents you with an interface to select the packages you wish to install.

1. Click on the Android Platform Tools entry in the left-most column.
2. Click the Accept radio button below the description in the right-most column.
3. Accept the Google USB Driver Package by clicking the OK button.
4. Optionally, reject the other packages. This saves some download time.
5. Click the Install button at the bottom of the SDK Manager.

   The selected SDK packages will download and install. When the download and installation process is complete, you can close the archive downloader and the SDK Manager.

At this point, the SDK platform tools (such as ADB, DDMS and others) should be installed on your computer. To verify this, follow these steps:

1. Open a command prompt window. (On Windows, press the Windows key+R. A run box will pop up. Type cmd and press Enter.)
2. In the command prompt window, you should see a path such as C:\Users\<username> followed by a flashing cursor. The cursor indicates where your typed text will show up. The path is the folder context in which you are issuing commands. In other words, every command typed at this prompt will attempt to run and affect the folder at C:\Users\<username>.
3. Click in the command prompt window, type cd \, and press Enter.

   The DOS command cd stands for "change directory". The backslash is shorthand for "the root of this disk". So the command cd \ means "change the folder to the root (or highest level) in this disk." You can access any location from any folder using the target folder's full path. It is important to learn these concepts because they are shared with the Android operating system command prompt. You will use these commands frequently.

4. Type cd "\Program Files(x86)\Android\android-sdk-windows\" and press Enter.

   This is the path you noted when the SDK Manager was installing the SDK. Make sure you include the quotation marks. Whenever there is a space in your command, you need to enclose it in quotation marks. If you are using a 32-bit operating system, you will not have the (x86) part of the path.

5. Now that you are in the context of the `android-sdk-windows` folder, you can test to see if the files and folders for the developer tools are functioning. Type `dir` and press Enter. The listing of folders and files should include a folder called `platform-tools`. This is the folder in which the `ADB.exe` command lives.

> *The `dir` command gives a listing of the files and folders in the current folder context in the Windows command window. At the Android command line (and in Linux), you use the `ls` command.*

6. Type `cd platform-tools` and press Enter to change your context to the `platform-tools` folder.

7. Type `adb` and press Enter. You should see the ADB command help screen scroll past (see Figure A-3).

Figure A-3: The ADB help screen, which appears when you run ADB with no switches or parameters

SETTING UP WINDOWS ENVIRONMENT VARIABLES

Now that you know that ADB is installed, you need to place a PATH entry in your system variables. This will enable you to use the ADB command regardless of the current folder context of your command prompt. For example, you want to be able to run the following command from the folder to which you have downloaded a custom TCP/IP module for your Android device:

```
adb push tcpip.ko \system\etc
```

If you do not do this, you will always need to be in the `c:\Program Files (x86)\Android\android-sdk-windows\platform-tools\` folder to run ADB.

To make the ADB command universally accessible (in Windows Vista and Windows 7), follow these steps:

1. Click the Windows Start button.
2. Right-click Computer and select Properties.
3. Click Advanced System Settings in the left column to open the System Properties dialog box.
4. Click the Environment Variables button.
5. In the System Variables box, scroll down until you see an entry labeled PATH.
6. Double-click the PATH entry to open the Edit variable window.
7. Click in the Variable Value field and place your cursor at the very end of the string of text.
8. Type a semi-colon (;).
9. Type in the full path to your ADB command folder: `C:\Program Files (x86)\Android\android-sdk-windows\platform-tools`.
10. Click on OK to close each of the open dialog boxes and close the System Properties box.

You should now be able to access ADB from a command line prompt, no matter which folder context your command line is in. This can be very useful if you are in the process of transferring exploit files from the folder into which you downloaded or extracted them.

Index